FIVE SCOTTISH
ONE-ACT PLAYS

Five Scottish One-Act Plays

Selected with Introduction and Notes

by

ROBERT MILLAR, M.A.
Moray House College of Education

and

J. T. LOW, B.A., Ph.D.
Moray House College of Education

HEINEMANN EDUCATIONAL BOOKS
LONDON AND EDINBURGH

Heinemann Educational Books Ltd
LONDON EDINBURGH MELBOURNE AUCKLAND TORONTO
SINGAPORE HONG KONG KUALA LUMPUR
NAIROBI IBADAN JOHANNESBURG
LUSAKA NEW DELHI

ISBN 0 435 23620 2

Introduction and Notes © Robert Millar and J. T. Low 1972
First published 1972
Reprinted 1974

Published by
Heinemann Educational Books Ltd
48 Charles Street, London W1X 8AH
Printed Offset Litho and bound in Great Britain by
Cox & Wyman Ltd, London, Fakenham and Reading

Contents

Acknowledgements

The editors and publisher wish to thank the following for permission to reprint the plays: Thomas Nelson and Sons Ltd for *Campbell of Kilmohr* by J. A. Ferguson; Hope Leresche and Steele Ltd for *Thread o' Scarlet* from *One-Act Plays* by J. J. Bell; Curtis Brown Ltd for *Rory Aforesaid* by John Brandane and *The Pardoner's Tale* by James Bridie; J. Garnet Miller Ltd for *Hewers of Coal* by Joe Corrie.

Preface

The study of Scottish literature in schools, and especially that part of it written for the stage, has been hampered by the lack of texts easily accessible and at a reasonable price.

The present volume seeks to remedy this for one form of drama by bringing together five Scottish one-act plays that are of the highest merit, judged by any standards. They were all written during that exciting period from 1909 to 1939 when, for the first time, a Scottish theatrical tradition was being established, mainly by the efforts of the Glasgow Repertory Theatre, then the Scottish National Players and, on the amateur side, the Scottish Community Drama Association.

The form taken by the book results from two main aims, both concerned with giving pupils an opportunity of meeting the best work of the best Scottish writers in this field of drama. The first is to encourage them to look at the plays as printed pieces that have to be translated into dialogue and action on a stage. To this end various guide lines are provided whereby the plays may be produced for enjoyment in class or for performances before a wider audience. The second is to show the scripts as examples of a specific literary genre in which a situation is worked out by human beings in terms of thought, feeling and action, and in which the technique that informs the one-acter can be observed and appreciated through the close study of superb examples of their kind.

But even if close study is not undertaken, the plays are offered as pleasurable class reading that has the power to fire the mind and stir the blood.

R.M.
J.T.L.

Introduction: How A One-Act Play Works

Before looking closely at the structure of a one-act play, let us remember that it was only at the beginning of the twentieth century that, after hundreds of years of neglect, this dramatic form was given serious treatment by professional dramatists, producers, and actors. To understand this renewed interest, we have to look at the conditions in the early years of the century. Outside of London, theatres depended for their shows largely on touring companies formed to exploit successes on the west-end stage; and almost every town of any size had a live theatre assured of responsive audiences.

Because of this general interest and the influence of educated audiences, there was a basis for the establishment in provincial cities of local theatres that could cater for local tastes and encourage local dramatists. Such groups as the Abbey Theatre in Dublin (1904), the Manchester Repertory Theatre (1907), the Pilgrim Players (1907) (who later became the Birmingham Repertory Theatre in 1913), and the Glasgow Repertory Theatre (1909), were more receptive to the staging of one-act plays; and the demand stimulated the supply. In the years following World War I the professional theatre was complemented by the amateur enthusiasts of the British Drama League in England and the Scottish Community Drama Association, whose member clubs in cities, towns and villages largely existed on a diet of one-act plays, some specially written for the local situation and group. With all this provincial activity, playwrights became more and more aware of the particular problems inherent in the creation of a good one-acter and in the techniques by which the problems could be solved. It was in this way that a whole literature of one-act plays came into being.

The one-act play, by exploiting a single dramatic situation, has in a short space of time to provide a complete theatrical experience. It has little time to elaborate and embroider: it must outline briefly, come to its climax swiftly, and end forcefully. As with other literary forms there are accepted rules governing dramatic structure. A play has certain well-defined sections or landmarks. It must have an *exposition* in which the situation is set forth and in which the main characters are introduced; *complications* leading to a conflict of interest and a whipping up of action and tension; a great *climax* marking the crisis of the action and tension; and a *dénouement* or conclusion providing the solution or indicating the consequences of the action. We cannot say that all five one-act plays in this book fit into this pattern exactly: each play has its own variations and subtleties; but an appreciation of this basic four-part structure will help us to understand how these five plays work on the stage.

The opening section or movement in a one-act play frequently presents the atmosphere to be exploited as well as the exposition. In *Campbell of Kilmohr* we immediately become aware of the wild weather outside and the life-and-death importance of the signal – the light in the window that means safety for the fugitive Dugald. In *The Pardoner's Tale*, out of the misery of the night comes Elliot (Life) vigorously seeking shelter and drink, in sharp contrast to the Old Man (Death) calm, withdrawn. The exposition is not always restricted to the first sequence: in *Thread o' Scarlet* it is continued and developed in later sequences.

One is aware in the one-act play of a fairly quick build-up to the complications. In *Rory Aforesaid* these come as a quarrel between MacCallum and MacIntosh – a kind of preliminary to the actual trial. In *Campbell of Kilmohr* the complications develop first in Campbell's interrogation of Dugald and then in his interrogation of Mary Stewart who almost destroys his self-assurance. In *The Pardoner's Tale* the complications build up through two narrations – Philip's story of Andrew and the Old Man's story of the Bains – to the finding of the treasure box by Elliot. In *Thread o' Scarlet* the complications reach high points with the entry of the Traveller and his tale of the strange man he had encountered. In *Hewers of Coal* the conflicts between Dick and Peter over the 'piece', and between Dick and Bob over the state of the mine, are clear examples of complications. It is important in production to shape these by flow and pace; but the strongest emphasis must be kept for the climaxes.

Somewhere – three-quarters through the play or (in a one-act play) very near the end – comes the big climax. In *Campbell of Kilmohr* this is the more effective for beginning at a slack point in the pace where Campbell has practically lost hope and where Morag gradually comes back into focus. From here the play builds up to the dramatic moment when she gives away the secret. This is a subtle climax too, for it is in a sense a false one: Campbell goes off believing he has won. In *Rory Aforesaid* the big climax comes in two parts: it is anticipated in the conspiracy scene where Rory decides to act a sheep, and it is played out in the trial scene where he actually plays the part. In *Hewers of Coal* the climax – the explosion and entombment – is dependent on external effects and comes at the height of the conflict between Dick and Bob. In *The Pardoner's Tale* the climax is also external in the sense that the intrigue against Philip ends with the physical action of the stabbing. In *Thread o' Scarlet* the climax begins with Breen's final entry and builds up to the revealing of the money-bag and the scarlet muffler: it is a good example of a climax which deceives and fuses into a surprise conclusion.

It is perhaps in the conclusion that the one-act play differs most from the full-length play. True, we sometimes find an almost traditional unravelling or dénouement along with the emphasizing of the lesson or the high theme. Mary Stewart's final speech in *Campbell of Kilmohr* is a good example of how the whole tone can be heightened by a powerful speech of explanation which by universalizing the theme strengthens the tragic quality of the play. *Thread o' Scarlet* exploits the surprise ending in typical *Grand Guignol* manner; it concludes with a spine-chilling twist. The ends are apparently all tied up neatly in the final Breen-Traveller sequence, only to be undone by Butters's final act – his blundering accusation. *The Pardoner's Tale* relies for the effect of its final scene purely on the visual – the look of horror on the faces of Elliot and Grant as they realize they have been poisoned. The conclusion of *Rory Aforesaid* exploits a genuinely comic device: the trick used in the central climactic scene – Rory's acting the sheep – is turned against the intriguer so that Rory emerges doubly triumphant. In *Hewers of Coal*, as in *Campbell of Kilmohr*, the ending heightens the tragedy: Joe's death, starkly indicated by the text, is ironically counterpointed by the tapping noises of the people who are rescuing the entombed miners.

If we pay attention to these aspects of the dramatic shape of the plays we shall the better be able to understand their drift and the better able to present them on the stage, whether in the classroom or in the school hall. When we come to study full-length plays, whether by Shakespeare or more modern writers, we shall be better prepared to consider them as plays if we think in terms of their dramatic shape – their expositions, complications, conflicts, climaxes, tensions, and the effect of their concluding scenes. A play can only work properly on the stage; and the one-act play, by reason of its swifter build-up and more concentrated dramatic power, should prove ideal for the classroom stage. In addition, the Scottish qualities of these plays – their starkness, their historical colour, their earthiness, their vigour – should appeal to Scottish pupils, and may also have for English and other non-Scottish pupils the attractiveness that the foreign or the exotic or even the out-landish holds for us all.

Campbell of Kilmohr

A Tragedy in One Act

by

J. A. FERGUSON

John A. Ferguson (1873–19   ), poet as well as playwright, became caught up in the enthusiasm generated by the Scottish Repertory Theatre, which during its existence from 1909 to 1914 had in its ranks some of the most brilliant actors and actresses of the day. Of the few contributions made by Scots writers to its repertoire, *Campbell of Kilmohr* was outstanding. It was given its first performance in March, 1914, at the Royalty Theatre, Glasgow. The acclaim given to it provided inspiration for Scots dramatists after World War I. It is marked by clear characterization, the inexorable progress of the action, a controlled use of suspense and atmosphere, and an ending of truly tragic power. The text used here is the one the author wanted to be taken as his final acting version.

PERSONS IN THE PLAY

In order of appearance

MARY STEWART
MORAG CAMERON
DUGALD STEWART
CAPTAIN SANDEMAN
ARCHIBALD CAMPBELL
JAMES MACKENZIE

SCENE: *Interior of a lonely cottage on the road from Struan to Rannoch, in North Perthshire.*

TIME: *1746, just after the collapse of the '45 Rebellion.*

SET

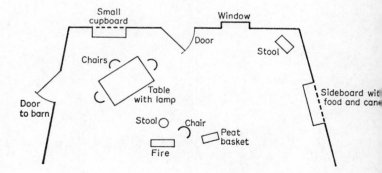

CAMPBELL OF KILMOHR

MORAG *is restlessly moving backwards and forwards. The old woman is seated on a low stool beside the peat fire in the centre of the floor.*

The room is scantily furnished and the women are poorly clad. MORAG *is barefooted. At the back is the door that leads to the outside. On the left of the door is a small window. On the right side of the room there is a door that opens into a barn.* MORAG *stands for a moment at the window, looking out.*

MORAG: It is the wild night outside.

MARY STEWART: Is the snow still coming down?

MORAG: It is that then – dancing and swirling with the wind too, and never stopping at all. Aye, and so black I cannot see the other side of the road.

MARY STEWART: That is good.

(MORAG *moves across the floor and stops irresolutely. She is restless, expectant.*)

MORAG: Will I be putting the light in the window?

MARY STEWART: Why should you be doing that! You have not heard his call (*turns eagerly*), have you?

MORAG (*with sign of head*): No, but the light in the window would show him all is well.

MARY STEWART: It would not then! The light was to be put there *after* we had heard the signal.

MORAG: But on a night like this he may have been calling for long and we never hear him.

MARY STEWART: Do not be so anxious, Morag. Keep to what he says. Put more peat on the fire now and sit down.

MORAG (*with increasing excitement*): I canna, I canna! There is that in me that tells me something is going to befall us this night. Oh, that wind, hear to it, sobbing round the house as if it brought some poor lost soul up to the door, and we refusing it shelter.

MARY STEWART: Do not be fretting yourself like that. Do as I bid you. Put more peats to the fire.

MORAG (*at the wicker peat-basket*): Never since I . . . What was that? (*Both listening for a moment.*)

MARY STEWART: It was just the wind; it is rising more. A sore night for them that are out in the heather.

(MORAG *puts peat on the fire without speaking.*)

MARY STEWART: Did you notice were there many people going by today?

MORAG: No. After daybreak the redcoats came by from Struan: and there was no more till nine, when an old man like the Catechist from Killichonan passed. At four o'clock, just when the dark was falling, a horseman with a lad holding to the stirrup, and running fast, went by towards Rannoch.

MARY STEWART: But no more redcoats?

MORAG (*shaking her head*): The road has been as quiet as the hills, and they as quiet as the grave. Do you think he will come?

MARY STEWART: Is it you think I have the gift, girl, that you ask me that? All I know is that it is five days since he was here for meat and drink for himself and for the others – five days and five nights, mind you; and little enough he took away; and those in hiding no' used to sore lying I'll be thinking. He must try to get through tonight. But that quietness, with no one to be seen from daylight till dark, I do not like it, Morag. They must know something. They must be watching.

(*A sound is heard by both women. They stand listening.*)

MARY STEWART: Haste you with the light, Morag.

MORAG: But it came from the back of the house – from the hillside.

MARY STEWART: Do as I tell you. The other side may be watched.

(*A candle is lit and placed in the window.* GIRL *goes hurrying to the door.*)

MARY STEWART: Stop, stop! Would you be opening the door with a light like that shining from the house? A man would be seen against it in the doorway for a mile. And who knows what eyes may be watching? Put out the light now and cover the fire.

(*Room is reduced to semi-darkness, and the door unbarred. Someone enters.*)

MORAG: You are cold, Dugald!

(STEWART, *very exhausted, signs assent.*)

MORAG: And wet, oh, wet through and through!

STEWART: Erricht Brig was guarded, well guarded. I had to win across the water.

(*The* OLD WOMAN *has now relit candle and taken away plaid from fire.*)

MARY STEWART: Erricht Brig – then—

STEWART (*nods*): Yes – in a corrie, on the far side of Dearig, half-way up.

MARY STEWART: Himself is there then?

STEWART: Aye, and Keppoch as well, and another and a greater is with them.

MARY STEWART: Wheest! (*Glances at Morag.*)

STEWART: Mother, is it that you can . . .

MARY STEWART: Yes, yes, Morag will bring out the food for ye to carry back. It is under the hay in the barn, well hid. Morag will bring it. Go, Morag, and bring it.

(MORAG *enters other room or barn which opens on right.*)

STEWART: Mother, I wonder at ye; Morag would never tell – never.

MARY STEWART: Morag is only a lass yet. She has never been tried. And who knows what she might be made to tell.

STEWART: Well, well, it is no matter, for I was telling you where I left them, but not where I am to *find* them.

MARY STEWART: They are not where you said now?

STEWART: No; they left the corrie last night, and I am to find them (*whispers*) in a quiet part on Rannoch Moor.

MARY STEWART: It is well for a young lass not to be knowing. Do not tell her.

STEWART: Well, well, I will not tell her. Then she cannot tell where they are even if she wanted to.

(*He sits down at table; the* OLD WOMAN *ministers to his wants.*)

STEWART: A fire is a merry thing on a night like this; and a roof over the head is a great comfort.

MARY STEWART: Ye'll no' can stop the night?

STEWART: No. I must be many a mile from here before the day breaks on Ben Dearig.

(MORAG *re-enters.*)

MORAG: It was hard to get through, Dugald?

STEWART: You may say that. I came down Erricht for three miles, and then when I reached low country I had to take to walking in the burns because of the snow that shows a man's steps and tells who he is to them that can read; and there's plenty can do that abroad, God knows.

MORAG: But none spied ye?

STEWART: Who can tell? Before dark came, from far up on the slopes of Dearig I saw soldiers down below; and away towards Rannoch Moor they were scattered all over the country like black flies on a white sheet. A wild-cat or anything that couldna fly could never have got through. And men at every brig and ford and pass! I had to strike away up across the slopes again; and even so as I turned round the bend beyond Kilrain I ran straight into a sentry sheltering behind a great rock. But after all that it was easy going.

MORAG: How could that be?

STEWART: Well, you see, I took the boots off him, and then I had no need to mind who might see my steps in the snow.

MORAG: You took the boots off him!

STEWART (*laughing*): I did that same. Does that puzzle your bonny head? How does a lad take the boots off a redcoat? Find out the answer, my lass, while I will be finishing my meat.

MORAG: Maybe he was asleep?

STEWART: Asleep! Asleep! Well, well, he sleeps sound enough now, with the ten toes of him pointed to the sky.

(*The* OLD WOMAN *has taken up dirk from table. She puts it down again.* MORAG *sees the action, and pushes dirk away so that it rolls off the table and drops to the floor. She hides her face in her hands.*)

MARY STEWART: Morag, bring in the kebbuck o' cheese. Now that all is well and safe it is we that will look after his comfort tonight. (MORAG *goes into barn.*) I mind well her mother saying to me – it was one day in the black winter that she died, when the frost took the land in its grip and the birds fell stiff from the trees, and the deer came down and put their noses to the door – I mind well her saying just before she died—

(*Loud knocking at the door.*)

A VOICE: In the King's name! (*Both rise, startled.*)

MARY STEWART (*recovering first*): The hay in the barn – quick my son.

(*Knocking continues.*)

A VOICE: Open in the King's name!

(STEWART *snatches up such articles as would reveal his presence and hurries into barn. He overlooks dirk on floor. The* OLD WOMAN *goes towards door, slowly, to gain time.*)

MARY STEWART: Who is there? What do you want?

A VOICE: Open, open.

(MARY STEWART *opens door, and* CAMPBELL OF KILMOHR *follows* CAPTAIN SANDEMAN *into the house. Behind Kilmohr comes a man carrying a leather wallet,* JAMES MACKENZIE, *his clerk. The rear is brought up by soldiers carrying arms.*)

SANDEMAN: Ha, the bird has flown.

CAMPBELL (*who has struck dirk with his foot and picked it up*): But the nest is warm; look at this.

SANDEMAN: It seems as if we had disturbed him at supper. Search the house, men.

MARY STEWART: I'm just a lonely old woman. You have been misguided. I was getting through my supper.

CAMPBELL (*holding up dirk*): And this was your toothpick, eh? Na! na! We ken whaur we are, and wha we want, and, by Cruachan, I think we've got him.

(*Sounds are heard from barn, and soldiers return with* MORAG. *She has stayed in hiding from fear, and she still holds the cheese in her hands.*)

SANDEMAN: What have we here!

CAMPBELL: A lass!

MARY STEWART: It's just my dead brother's daughter. She was getting me the cheese, as you can see.

CAMPBELL: On men, again: the other turtle-doo will no' be far away. (*Bantering, to the old woman.*) Tut, tut, Mistress Stewart, and do ye have her wait upon ye while your leddyship dines alane! A grand way to treat your dead brother's daughter; fie, fie upon ye!

(SOLDIERS *reappear with Stewart, whose arms are pinioned.*)

CAMPBELL: Did I no' tell ye! And this, Mrs Stewart, will be your dead sister's son, I'm thinking; or aiblins your leddyship's butler! Weel, woman, I'll tell ye this: Pharaoh spared ae butler, but Erchie Campbell will no spare anither. Na! na! Pharaoh's case is no' to be taken as forming ony preceedent. And so if he doesna answer certain questions we have to speir at him, before morning he'll hang as high as Haman. (STEWART *is placed before the table at which Campbell has seated himself.* TWO SOLDIERS *guard Stewart. Another is behind Campbell's chair and another is by the door. The clerk,* MACKENZIE, *is seated at up corner of table.* SANDEMAN *stands by the fire.*)

CAMPBELL (*to Stewart*): Weel, sir, it is within the cognizance of the law that you have knowledge and information of the place of harbour and concealment used by certain persons who are in a state of proscription. Furthermore, it is known that four days ago certain other proscribed persons did join with these, and that they are banded together in an endeavour to secure the escape from these dominions of His Majesty, King George, of certain persons who by their crimes and treasons lie open to the capital charge. What say ye?

(STEWART *makes no reply.*)

CAMPBELL: Ye admit this then?

(STEWART *as before.*)

CAMPBELL: Come, come, my lad. Ye stand in great jeopardy. Great affairs of state lie behind this which are beyond your simple understanding. Speak up, and it will be the better for ye.

(STEWART *silent as before.*)

CAMPBELL: Look you. I'll be frank with you. No harm will befall you this night (and I wish all in this house to note my words) – no harm will befall you this night if you supply the information required.

(STEWART *as before.*)

CAMPBELL (*with sudden passion*): Sandeman, put your sword to the carcass o' this muckle ass and see will it louse his tongue.

(SANDEMAN *does not move.*)

STEWART: It may be as well then, Mr Campbell, that I should say a word to save your breath. It is this: Till you talk Rannoch Loch to the top of Schiehallion ye'll no' talk me into a yea or nay.

CAMPBELL (*quietly*): Say ye so? Noo, I wadna be so very sure if I were you. I've had a lairge experience o' life and speaking out of it I would say that only fools and the dead never change their minds.

STEWART (*quietly too*): Then you'll be adding to your experience tonight, Mr Campbell, and you'll have something to put on the other side of it.

CAMPBELL (*tapping his snuff-box*): Very possibly, young sir, but what I would present for your consideration is this: While ye may be prepared to keep your mouth shut under the condition of a fool, are ye equally prepared to do so in the condition of a dead man?

(CAMPBELL *waits expectantly.* STEWART *silent as before.*)

CAMPBELL: Tut, tut, now if it's afraid ye are, my lad, with my hand on my heart and on my word as a gentleman . . .

STEWART: Afraid!

(*He spits in contempt towards Campbell.*)

CAMPBELL (*enraged*): Ye damned stubborn Hieland stot . . . (*To Sandeman.*) Have him taken out. We'll get it another way.

(CAMPBELL *rises.* STEWART *is moved into barn by soldiers, who remain with him.*)

CAMPBELL (*walking*): Some puling eediots, Sandeman, would applaud this contumacy and call it constancy. Constancy! Now, I've had a lairge experience o' life, and I never saw yet a sensible man insensible to the touch of yellow metal. If there may be such a man, it is demonstrable that he is no sensible man. Fideelity! quotha, it's sheer obstinacy. They just see that ye want something oot o' them, and they're so damned selfish and thrawn they winna pairt. And with the

natural inabeelity o' their brains to hold mair than one idea
at a time, they canna see that in return you could put something into their palms far more profitable. (*Sits again at table.*)
Aweel, bring Mistress Stewart up.

(OLD WOMAN *is placed before him where son had been.*)

CAMPBELL (*more ingratiatingly*): Weel noo, Mistress Stewart,
good woman, this is a sair predeecament for yet to be in. I
would jist counsel ye to be candid. Doubtless yer mind is a'
in a swirl. Ye kenna what way to turn. Maybe ye are like
the Psalmist and say: 'I lookit this way and that, and there
was no man to peety me, or to have compassion upon my
fatherless children.' But, see now, ye would be wrong; and,
if ye tell me a'ye ken, I'll stand freends wi' ye. Put your trust
in Erchie Campbell.

MARY STEWART: I trust no Campbell.

CAMPBELL: Weel, weel, noo, I'm no' jist that set up wi' them
myself. There's but ae Campbell that I care muckle aboot,
after a'. But, good wife, it's no' the Campbells we're trying
the noo; so, as time presses, we'll jist *birze yont*, as they say
themselves. Noo then, speak up.

(MARY STEWART *is silent.*)

CAMPBELL (*beginning grimly and, passing through astonishment,
expostulation, and a feigned contempt for mother and pity for son,
to a pretence of sadness which, except at the end, makes his words
come haltingly*): Ah! ye also. I suppose ye understand,
woman, how it will go wi' your son? (*To his clerk.*) Here's a
fine mother for ye, James! Would you believe it? She kens
what would save her son – the very babe she nursed at her
breast; but will she save him? Na! na! Sir, he may look after
himself! A mother, a mother! Ha! ha!

(CAMPBELL *laughs.* MACKENZIE *titters foolishly.* CAMPBELL
pauses to watch effect of his words.)

Aye, you would think, James, that she would remember
the time when he was but little and afraid of all the terrors

that walk in darkness, and how he looked up to her as to a tower of safety, and would run to her with outstretched hands, hiding his face from his fear, in her gown. The darkness! It is the dark night and a long journey before him now.

(*He pauses again.*)

You would think, James, that she would mind how she happit him from the cold of winter and sheltered him from the summer heats, and, when he began to find his footing, how she had an eye on a' the beasts of the field, and on the water and the fire that were become her enemies. And to what purpose all this care? – tell me that, my man, to what good, if she is to leave him at the last to dangle from a tree at the end of a hempen rope – to see his flesh to be meat for the fowls of the air – her son, her little son!

MARY STEWART (*softly*): My son – my little son! . . . Oh, (*more loudly*) but my son he has done no crime.

CAMPBELL: Has he no'? Weel, mistress, as ye'll no' take my word for it, maybe ye'll list to Mr Mackenzie here. What say ye, James?

MACKENZIE: He is guilty of aiding and abetting in the concealment of proscribed persons; likewise with being found in the possession of arms, contrary to statute, both very heinous crimes.

CAMPBELL: Very well said, James! Forby, between ourselves, Mrs Stewart, the young man in my opeenion is guilty of another crime (*snuffs*) – he is guilty of the heinous crime of not knowing on which side his bread is buttered. Come now. . . .

MARY STEWART: Ye durst not lay a finger on the lad, ye durst not hang him.

MACKENZIE: And why should the gentleman not hang him if it pleesure him?

(CAMPBELL *taps snuff-box and takes pinch.*)

MARY STEWART (*with intensity*): Campbell of Kilmohr, lay but one finger on Dugald Stewart and the weight of Ben Cruachan will be light to the weight that will be laid on your soul. I will lay the curse of the seven rings upon your life. I will call up the fires of Ephron, the blue and the green and the grey fires, for the destruction of your soul. I will curse you in your homestead and in the wife it shelters, and in the children that will never bear your name. Yea and ye shall be cursed.

CAMPBELL (*startled, betrays agitation – the snuff is spilt from his trembling hand*): Hoot, toot, woman! ye're, ye're . . . (*Angrily.*) Ye auld beldame, to say such things to me! I'll have ye first whippit and syne droont for a witch. Damn thae stubborn and supersteetious cattle! (*To Sandeman.*) We should have come in here before him and listened in the barn, Sandeman!

SANDEMAN (*in quick staccato, always cool*): Ah, listen behind the door you mean! Now I never thought of that!

CAMPBELL: Did ye not! Humph! Well, no doubt there are a good many things in the universe that yet wait for your thought upon them. What would be your objections, now?

SANDEMAN: There are two objections, Kilmohr, that you would understand.

CAMPBELL: Name them.

SANDEMAN: Well, in the first place, we have not wings like crows to fly . . . and the footsteps on the snow. . . . Second point: the woman would have told him we were there.

CAMPBELL: Not if I told her I had the power to clap her in Inverness jail.

MARY STEWART (*in contempt*): Yes, even if ye had told me ye had power to clap me in hell, Mr Campbell.

CAMPBELL: Lift me that screeching Jezebel oot o' here; Sandeman, we'll mak' a quick finish o' this. (SOLDIERS *take her towards barn.*) No, not there, pitch the old girzie into the snow.

MARY STEWART (*as she is led outside*): Ye'll never find him, Campbell, never, never!

CAMPBELL (*enraged*): Find him, aye, by God I'll find him, if I have to keek under every stone on the mountains from the Boar of Badenoch to the Sow of Athole. (OLD WOMAN *and* SOLDIERS *go outside, leaving only* CAMPBELL, MACKENZIE, SANDEMAN, *and* MORAG *in the room;* MORAG *huddled up on stool.*) And now, Captain Sandeman, you an' me must have a word or two. I noted your objection to listening ahint doors and so on. Now, I make a' necessary allowances for youth and the grand and magneeficent ideas commonly held, for a little while, in that period. I had them myself. But, man, gin ye had trod the floor of the Parliament Hoose in Edinburry as long as I did, wi' a pair o' thin hands at the bottom o' toom pockets, ye'd ha'e shed your fine notions, as I did. Noo, fine pernickety noansense will no' do in this business—

SANDEMAN: Sir!

CAMPBELL: Softly, softly, Captain Sandeman, and hear till what I have to say. I have noticed with regret several things in your remarks and bearing which are displeasing to me. I would say just one word in your ear; it is this: These things, Sandeman, are not conducive to advancement in His Majesty's service.

SANDEMAN (*after a brief pause in which the two eye each other*): Kilmohr, I am a soldier, and if I speak out my mind you must pardon me if my words are blunt: I do not like this work, but I *loathe* your methods.

CAMPBELL: Mislike the methods you may, but the work ye must do! Methods are my business. Let me tell you the true position. In ae word it is no more and no less than this. You and me are baith here to carry out the proveesions of the

Act for the Pacification of the Highlands. That means the cleaning up of a very big mess, Sandeman, a very big mess. Now, what is your special office in this work? I'll tell ye, man; you and your men are just beesoms in the hands of the law-officers of the Crown. In this district, I order and ye soop. (*He indicates door of barn.*) Now soop, Captain Sandeman.

SANDEMAN: What are you after? I would give something to see into your mind.

CAMPBELL: Ne'er fash aboot my mind: what has a soldier to do with ony mental operations? It's His Grace's orders that concerns you. Oot wi' your man and set him up against the wa'.

SANDEMAN: Kilmohr, it is murder – murder, Kilmohr!

CAMPBELL: Hoots awa', man, it's a thing o' nae special signeeficence.

SANDEMAN: I must ask you for a warrant.

CAMPBELL: Quick, then: Mackenzie will bring it out to you. (CLERK *begins writing as* SANDEMAN *goes and orders the soldiers to lead Stewart outside.* CAMPBELL *sits very still and thoughtful.* CLERK *finishes writing and places warrant. before Campbell for his signature.*)

MACKENZIE: At this place, sir.

CAMPBELL (*again alert*): Hoots, I was forgetting.

MACKENZIE: It is a great power ye have in your hands, Kilmohr, to be able to send a man to death on the nod, as ye might say.

CAMPBELL (*sitting back, pen in hand*): Power! power say ye? Man, do ye no' see I've been beaten. Do ye no' see that? Archibald Campbell and a' his men and his money are less to them than the wind blowing in their faces.

MACKENZIE: Well, it's a strange thing that.

CAMPBELL (*throwing down the pen and rising*): Aye, it's a strange thing that. It's a thing fit to sicken a man against the notion that there are probabilities on this earth. . . . Ye see, James, beforehand I would have said nothing could be easier.

MACKENZIE: Than to get them to tell?

CAMPBELL: Aye, just that. But you heard what he said: 'You'll be adding to your experience this night, Mr Campbell, and you'll have something to put to the other side of it,' says he. (*Paces away, hands behind back.*) Aye, and I have added something to it, a thing I like but little. (*Turning to face Mackenzie with raised hand.*) Do you see what it is, James? A dream can be stronger than a strong man armed. Just a whispered word, a pointed finger even, would ha'e tell'd us a'. But no! no! And so I am powerless before the visions and dreams of an old woman and a half-grown lad.

MACKENZIE (*who now stands waiting for the warrant*): No' exactly powerless, Kilmohr, for if ye canna open his mouth ye can shut it; and there's some satisfaction in that.

CAMPBELL (*sitting down to sign warrant*): No' to me, man, no' to me. (*He hands the paper to Mackenzie, who goes out.*) For I've been beaten. Aye, the pair o' them have beat me, though it's only a matter o' seconds till one o' them be dead.

MORAG (*her voice coming quickly, in a sharp whisper, like an echo of Campbell's last word as she sits up to stare at him*): Dead!

CAMPBELL (*startled*): What is that?

MORAG (*slowly*): Is he dead?

CAMPBELL (*aloud*): Oh, it's you. I'd forgotten you were there.

MORAG (*in same tone*): Is he dead?

CAMPBELL (*grimly*): Not yet. But if ye'll look through this window preesently ye'll see him gotten ready for death.

(*He picks up hat, gloves, cloak, and is about to go out.*)

MORAG (*after a pause, very slowly and brokenly*): I – will – tell – you.

CAMPBELL (*astounded*). What!

MORAG: I will tell you all you are seeking to know.

CAMPBELL (*in a whisper, thunderstruck*): God, and to think, to think I was on the very act . . . on the very act of . . . (*Recovering.*) Tell me – tell me at once.

MORAG: You will promise that he will not be hanged?

CAMPBELL: He will not. I swear it.

MORAG: You will give him back to me?

CAMPBELL: I will give him back – unhung.

MORAG: Then (CAMPBELL *comes near*), in a corrie half-way up the far side of Dearig – God save me!

CAMPBELL (*in exultation*): Dished after a'. I've clean dished them! Loard, Loard! (*With intense solemnity, clasping hands and looking upwards.*) Once more I can believe in the rationality of Thy world. (*Gathers up again his cloak, hat, etc.*) And to think . . . to think . . . I was on the very act of going away like a beaten dog!

MORAG: He is safe from hanging now?

CAMPBELL (*chuckles and looks out at window before replying, and is at door when he speaks*): Very near it, very near it. Listen! (*He holds up his hand – a volley of musketry is heard.* KILMOHR *goes out, leaving door wide open. After a short interval of silence, the* OLD WOMAN *enters and advances a few steps towards the girl, who has sunk on her knees at the volley.*)

MARY STEWART: Did you hear, Morag Cameron, did you hear?

(*The* GIRL *is sobbing, her face covered by her hands.*)

MARY STEWART: Och! be quiet now. I would be listening till the last sound of it passes into the great hills and over all the wide world. . . . It is fitting for you to be crying, a child that cannot understand, but water shall never wet eye of mine for Dugald Stewart. Last night I was but the mother of a lad that herded sheep on the Athole hills: this morn it is I that am the mother of a man who is among the great ones of the earth. All over the land they will be telling of Dugald Stewart. Mothers will teach their children to be men by

him. High will his name be with the teller of fine tales. . . .
The great men came, they came in their pride, terrible like
the storm they were, and cunning with the words of guile
were they. Death was with them. . . . He was but a lad, a
young lad, with great length of days before him, and the
grandeur of the world. But he put it all from him. 'Speak,'
said they, 'speak, and life and great riches will be for yourself.'
But he said no word at all! Loud was the swelling of their
wrath! Let the heart of you rejoice, Morag Cameron, for
the snow is red with his blood. There are things greater than
death. Let them that are children shed the tears. . . .

(*She comes forward and lays her hand on the girl's shoulder.*)

MARY STEWART: Let us go and lift him into the house, and
not be leaving him lie out there alone.

CURTAIN

GLOSSARY

aiblins: perhaps
besom: (a) broom
birze yont: press on
forby: besides
(the) gift: second sight
girzie: old hag
kebbuck: (a) whole cheese
keek: peep
louse: loosen

muckle: much
puling: whining
quotha: said he
soop: sweep
speir at: ask
stot: stupid clumsy fellow
syne: next
thrawn: stubborn
toom: empty

PRODUCTION NOTES

This is a play with wonderful moments of suspense, powerful confrontations, and a sense of tragedy that builds up gradually to a supremely moving conclusion. At the opening, the producer, by skilful lighting effects, controlled storm noises, and a steady development of an urgent note in the dialogue, can swiftly suggest the atmosphere of flight, persecution, and loyalty to an already lost cause. We should feel both excitement and relief at Dugald's entry; and in the midst of the dialogue that follows we should be aware of the deadly seriousness behind Dugald's laughing remarks. The entry of Campbell and his men is beautifully timed in the text: the director should reflect this by equally careful timing in production, contrasting the quiet tones of Mary Stewart with the sudden knocking and the ringing tones of the voice outside. Entries and positions at this point must be exactly plotted; and the interrogation of Dugald by Campbell must be so staged and produced as to bring out the contrast between the harshness of Campbell and the calm loyalty of Dugald. In the second interrogation there must be a steady build-up of pace to the moment when Mary Stewart by her intensity and vehemence puts Campbell momentarily out of countenance. After such tension and high drama it might be difficult to maintain interest in the Campbell–Sandeman passage and in the Campbell–Mackenzie passage; but there is shape to be traced in each of these sequences and in Campbell's speeches. In the first pace builds up to 'Now soop, Captain Sandeman . . .'; in the second it slackens deliberately during Campbell's speech that ends: 'And so I am powerless before the visions and dreams . . .' As the author himself points out in his acting notes, we should be completely unaware of Morag during this scene, until she 'lifts her face and echoes Campbell's "Dead!"' And slowly but deliberately that dialogue between Campbell and Morag must take shape, observing two landmarks on the way – 'I – will – tell – you . . .', and '. . . in a corrie half-way up on the far side of Dearg . . .', and concluding with the volley of musketry. After Campbell's exit, movements must be quiet but deliberate: the girl's sobbing must not be allowed to spoil the effect of Mary Stewart's concluding speech; and that speech must be spoken clearly with intensity and power but without any ranting or dragging out of words. The tragedy must emerge in this speech and in the quiet humanity of Mary's very last words 'Let us go and lift him into the house'.

TALKING POINTS

On Staging and Acting

1. How would you direct those playing Dugald and Morag in the scene that features the dirk? Consider how the contrast between Dugald's gentle mockery and Morag's *naiveté* might be pointed, and how the manipulation of the dirk helps Morag to understand the full implications of Dugald's story.

2. By diagrams and notes show how you would stage the entry of Campbell and his men. Indicate the exact order of entry, and say where you would place the characters, including three or four soldiers.

3. Examine carefully the scene of Campbell's interrogation of Dugald Stewart. What contrasts in character, bearing, and speaking would you try to bring out in production and where?

4. How would you bring out the dramatic change in mood when Morag offers to give Campbell the information he is seeking? Where do you think Morag might have been placed during the previous scenes, and how would you *pace* the dramatic duologue that follows?

5. The author recommended that special care be given to Mary Stewart's final speech. Examine this speech closely, and then decide how it should be spoken on the stage. Add a comment on the dramatic effect of the final sentence uttered by Mary.

On the Human Situation

1. Sandeman says to Campbell, 'I loathe your methods'. How skilful were the methods and what do *you* find objectionable in them?
2. The tragedy demands that Campbell be beaten. Measure his success against his failure.
3. The play's theme is loyalty: loyalty to the Prince and loyalty to £30,000. Discuss the various aspects of these loyalties.
4. Tragedy asserts the greatness of the human spirit in the face of adversity. Consider the greatness of Mary Stewart.
5. Was Dugald brave or just foolish?

Thread O' Scarlet

A Thriller in One Act

by

J. J. BELL

James Joy Bell (1871–1934) was a prolific writer of varied talents. He is best known for his humorous writings collected under the title of *Wee Macgregor*, some of which, in the form of sketches, were put on by the Glasgow Repertory Theatre. His interest in and command of the vernacular, particularly that of Glasgow, made him a pioneer in the use of Scots for racy and comic dialogue. *Thread o' Scarlet* was written in 1923, reputedly at a single all night sitting from ten o'clock one night till four o'clock next morning. A fine piece of *Grand Guignol* theatre – a thriller – it is a swiftly moving play which hides its solution cleverly as the tension mounts to the curtain climax. As written it can be played using any kind of regional speech.

PERSONS IN THE PLAY

In order of appearance

MIGSWORTH ⎫
SMITH ⎬ *Village Tradesmen*
BUTTERS ⎭

LANDLORD *of Inn*
BREEN *an odd-job man*
A TRAVELLER

SCENE: *Smoke room of a Village Inn.*

TIME: *Twentieth Century up till 1965, when hanging was abolished as the penalty for murder.*

Applications regarding performances of this play should be addressed to Hope Leresche & Steele Ltd, 11 Jubilee Place, London S.W.3. No performance may be given unless permission has first been obtained.

SET

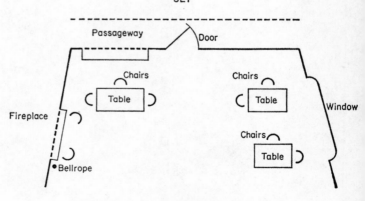

THREAD O' SCARLET

SCENE: *Smoke-room of a small village inn, some eight miles from the county town. Low ceiling. Broad window with screens* L. *Fire* R., *ruddy embers. Door opening on passage at back. Barely furnished. Several small tables with their complements of chairs. Crude old-fashioned oleographs on walls. Bell-rope at side of fireplace. An evening in February, about twenty minutes from closing time. A bitter wind is blowing outside, coming in squalls, with blatters of sleet against the window.*

TIME: *The present.*

MIGSWORTH, SMITH, *and* BUTTERS *are seated at a table, tankards before them.* MIGSWORTH, *who fancies himself a bit superior intellectually, and* SMITH, *a genial, rather stupid person, are interested in what is passing at back.* BUTTERS *appears sunk in his own thoughts; he is a big, heavy man; throughout the play he has a semi-dazed look. The door is open; the* LANDLORD *is standing in the entrance as if to block it, and* BREEN *is seen in the passage beyond.*

LANDLORD (*in tone of finality*): No, Mr Breen, I can't serve ye, and my advice to you is to go home, and to bed!

BREEN! Haven't I told ye, ye'll get the money in the mornin'?

LANDLORD: Quite so. But that's not my point. I've got a licence to lose. In other words—

BREEN: Come on, gimme a bottle o' whisky!

LANDLORD: No! Ye've had enough.

BREEN: Damn ye!

(*Goes out.*)

(*His footfalls are heard going down passage, steadily, and then the slam of the front door. The* LANDLORD, *wiping his brow, comes into the room.*)

MIGSWORTH: Quite right, Mr Flett. He's had more'n enough.

SMITH: Queer, though, how steady he walks! Don't he, Butters?

BUTTERS (*as one awakening*): Who? Oh, Breen! I'm sick o' Breen. Never out o' my shop spyin' around and tryin' to get something' for nothin'. Was there tonight when I was closin'. Had to turn him out. (*Relapses.*)

LANDLORD: 'Tis his head, not his legs, that takes it all. To tell the truth, gentlemen, I'm afraid – not of, but *for* him. Trade's rotten bad, the Lord knows, but I swear I'd sooner be without Breen's custom. He's been hard at it for a solid month, and gettin' worse every day. Can't think when or where he earns the money. But you rang, gentlemen.

MIGSWORTH (*with a wave towards tankards*): Same again, please.

(LANDLORD *makes to collect tankards.*)

BUTTERS (*as if waking*): No more for me. Must be goin' home.

MIGSWORTH: Tut! ye need another. We all do, after what we've gone through today.

(BUTTERS *lets his tankard go.*)

And mind ye, Mr Flett, I don't wonder at Breen goin' it hard after all *he's* gone through – lost his only friend. Both shiftless chaps, but—

LANDLORD: True, true, Mr Migsworth. Still, I prefer to see a man drownin' his sorrows in moderation. (*Goes out with tankards.*)

MIGSWORTH: Ah, what a day. Longest I've ever known.

SMITH: Not so long as last night must ha' been to Jacob Forge.

BUTTERS (*without raising his head*): Last night – oh, my soul!

(*His friends glance at him.*)

SMITH: Aye, ye must ha' felt it, Butters, havin' been on the jury. Always wondered why ye didn't get out o' that. I believe ye could. (*More cheerfully.*) And yet, here's the three o' us, sittin' round this table for close on three hours, chattin' about 'most everything but the thing we're thinkin' on.

MIGSWORTH: Well, as two single men and a widower without offspring (*nods at Butters*), 'twouldn't be natural to sit alone in our houses, dumb, and thinkin' o' Jacob Forge, our neighbour – that was. I couldn't do it.

SMITH (*in a burst of emotion*): Oh, oh, to think that at eight o'clock this blessed – I mean cursed – mornin' Jacob Forge was hanged by – by the neck until he was—

(BUTTERS *makes a fluttering gesture of protest.*)

MIGSWORTH: 'Sh! No need for to go into details, Mr Smith. Forge has paid the penalty o' his crime, havin' been found guilty by a jury o' good men and true, includin' our friend and neighbour here, William Butters, who—

BUTTERS (*sitting up*): I must be gettin' home. 'Tis on my mind that I left the keys o' my safe on the counter and didn't lock up anything properly. Was too upset. (*Half rises and subsides.*)

MIGSWORTH: Don't you worry, Mr Butters. Your property's all right. Aye, we may pity Jacob Forge, though none o' us liked him; but we know he had a fair trial and full justice. Not that I'd ever ha' dreamed o' him bein' a murd—

BUTTERS: Don't say it! 'Tis too awful. Jacob was a strange man, and yet— (*Pause.*) And, of course, we found him guilty because o' the evidence.

SMITH: Of course! Because o' the evidence! But, this mornin', when I see the black flag goin' up – they did hoist it slow! – I says to myself—

MIGSWORTH: Was *you* there?

SMITH: Aye: I saw ye, too, all muffled up. 'Twas a cold

mornin', though. Was muffled up myself. And you, Mr Butters – I *thought* I saw ye, too.

BUTTERS (*bowing his head*): I went – to pray – to pray that the black flag – might never go up. Oh, my soul!

MIGSWORTH: Now, what do ye mean by that?

(LANDLORD *enters. There is a short pause while he sets the tankards on the table.*)

We're talkin' o' the melancholy episode o' this mornin', Mr Flett. (*Lays money on table.*)

LANDLORD: Ah, yes, yes. Very shockin' to be sure, very shockin'. (*Taking money.*) Thank 'ee, sir. I understood from his remarks that Mr Breen had been there.

SMITH: What? Him?

MIGSWORTH: How could he? – his only friend bein' hanged!

LANDLORD: He was talkin' o' puttin' a knife in the judge that sentenced Forge – and poisonin' all the jury!

SMITH: That's awful! He must be goin' crazy.

MIGSWORTH (*sagely*): When a man takes to Scotch, he's done!

SMITH (*with an attempt at humour*): Beggin' your pardon – but judgin' from Mister Breen's case, I should say he's never done!

MIGSWORTH: Oh, very good, very good! (*Laughs discreetly.*)

BUTTERS (*shuddering*): What if Breen is right?

MIGSWORTH: Right?

BUTTERS: About the judge. And what – what's to happen to the judge and jury, if we was all wrong?

LANDLORD (*puzzled*): What's all this, Mr Butters!

(BUTTERS *relapses without response.*)

MIGSWORTH (*confidentially*): Nerves, Mr Flett, just nerves.

LANDLORD: *I* see, *I* see! And I knows a little about 'em, too. Fact is, I'm a bit that way at the moment.

SMITH: How so? (*Eager to drink, nods to* MIGSWORTH.) Good health! (*Drinks.*)

LANDLORD: I've got a notion – a preminotion, if ye understand

what I mean, gentlemen – that our unfortunate friend
Breen'll come back tonight; and I don't like it.

MIGSWORTH: Ye'll have our support, Mr Flett – our moral
support – in refusin' him refreshment.

LANDLORD: Thank 'ee, sir, thank 'ee. I'm bound to refuse
him. There's my conscience to be considered—

SMITH: *And* your licence. Besides, most likely he's got no
money.

LANDLORD: True, Mr Smith.
(*Goes out.*)

SMITH: Come away, Butters! This is real good beer – make
ye sleep sound.

BUTTERS (*as if awakening*): I saw Breen there this mornin'.
Our mufflin's was nothin' to his. But I spied his face – my
God, shall I ever forget his face when the flag was goin' up
and—

SMITH (*eagerly*): What was it like?

MIGSWORTH: 'Sh! Mr Smith. Suppused with grief, no
doubt!

BUTTERS: 'Twas like a – a soul in torments.

MIGSWORTH: Seems to have some decent feelin's after all,
though I *have* doubted it when seein' him sittin' there
(*points towards corner*) night after night, drinkin' on his own.
(*Drinks.*) Shows how careful we should be in judgin' our
neighbours.

SMITH (*after a long pulls*): Ah, well, maybe there was more
real friendship 'twixt him and Forge than we thought.
They was both such terrible close chaps.
(*Motor horn is heard.*)
Hullo, goin' to stop here. (*Rises and goes to window.*) My!
I don't envy any man his car on a night like this! Black as
hell; sleet drivin' well-nigh level! Ugh! (*Shivers.*) Glad I
haven't far to go. (*Starts back from a vivid flare of lightning,
which is followed quickly by a frightful thunder-clap.*)

(BUTTERS, *with a cry, leaps and subsides trembling.*)

MIGSWORTH (*with feigned coolness*): Bit unexpected at this season, wasn't it? Why, Mr Butters, ye're lookin' sickish! No danger, ye know.

BUTTERS (*with emotion*): Oh, there's somethin' wrong in the world this night – some awful wickedness abroad – I'm feared to take the road now—

SMITH (*returning to table*): Come, come, this won't do at all! Take a good sup o' your beer. Give ye comfort. Ye should never ha' gone to the hangin' this mornin'.

BUTTERS (*still trembling*): I tell ye – in yon flash I saw Jacob Forge, and he was hung – hung on a scarlet thread.

(MIGSWORTH *and* SMITH *look at each other.*)

MIGSWORTH: Tut! Tut!

BUTTERS (*frantically*): Nothin' but a scarlet thread – and he was dead and starin' and his head all sideways – sorter smilin' to himself as if—

SMITH (*in a gasp*): Smilin'!

MIGSWORTH: Hush!

(*Door opens.* TRAVELLER *enters followed by* LANDLORD.)

TRAVELLER (*impatiently as he removes dripping wraps*): Oh, this will do. Have a bedroom fired for me, and another for my man. But first let me have a double Scotch, some boiling water, sugar and lemon. (*Goes to fire and stands chafing his hands.*)

LANDLORD: Yes, sir.

(*Goes out.*)

(*A pause, during which* MIGSWORTH *and* SMITH *glance at the* TRAVELLER *and at each other.* BUTTERS, *chin on chest, takes no notice. There has been a lull in the storm, but now comes a blast of wind with a violent blatter of hail.*)

SMITH (*starting*): Lord, what's that?

MIGSWORTH: Only hail. The thunder's brought it down.

(*Is about to address* TRAVELLER.)

BUTTERS (*dreamily*): Hung by a scarlet thread and smilin' – smilin' the smile o' (*voice almost fails*) an innocent man—

SMITH (*under his breath*): Oh, I say!

MIGSWORTH (*leaning over and patting* BUTTERS's *shoulder*): Don't you worry about it, old man. (*Winking to Smith.*) I doubt he must ha' been loadin' up before he came here. (*Clears throat and addresses Traveller.*) Terrible night, sir.

TRAVELLER (*turning*): Horrible! (*Drily yet courteously.*) I hope I am not intruding here. Only place with a fire going.

MIGSWORTH: Not at all, sir. 'Tis a public room, and, if 'twas private, ye'd be welcome on such a night.

TRAVELLER: Much obliged, I'm sure. (*Takes chair at hearth. Yawns. Produces case and selects a cigarette. Lights up while* MIGSWORTH *and* SMITH *watch him with interest.*) There's a village about here, isn't there?

MIGSWORTH: Two, sir. Lower Ashley and Upper Ashley. This inn is midway betwixt them.

TRAVELLER: If you reside here, perhaps you can tell me whether the population includes a person – a man – who is stone-deaf – possibly dumb also.

MIGSWORTH: Oh, no, sir.

SMITH (*hopefully*): But we've got a paralytic, sir.

TRAVELLER: H'm! This man was apparently bound for one of the Ashleys, and he gave my chauffeur and me the nerve-shock of our lives.

(LANDLORD *enters with tray; sets it on small table which he places conveniently for the Traveller.*)

MIGSWORTH (*respectfully*): How was that, sir?

TRAVELLER (*to* LANDLORD): Thanks. (*While he mixes toddy.*) Well, in the midst of a blizzard, the lamps showed him walking in the middle of the road. We kept sounding the horn, but he paid no attention. We slowed and my man was going to risk the ditch, when the fellow stepped aside, and

we carried on. Next moment he was back in the middle of
the road.

(*The* LANDLORD, *who has moved to the door, halts, listening.*)
It was the nearest thing! Of course we braked hard, but I
swear the bonnet touched him when the car stopped with a
jerk that, I thought, had finished her – and then the fellow
walked on without so much as turning his head. (*Sips
toddy.*)

MIGSWORTH: My gracious! did ever one hear the like o' that?
What did ye do, sir?

TRAVELLER: Shouted on him to stop, but he paid no attention. I think he must have left the road soon after, for when
we got going again – the car had suffered, you understand –
there was no sign of him. (*Savagely.*) I'd like very much to
get a word with him!

MIGSWORTH: Sounds like a lunatic, sir. And ye never saw his
face?

TRAVELLER: Nothing but his back. (*Sips.*) A biggish man, in a
long tarpaulin coat and a soft felt hat.

SMITH: Plenty o' tarpaulins and soft felts – old ones – here-
abouts.

TRAVELLER: He had a heavy muffler coming above the coat-
collar as if to shield the back of his head. I noted it in the
lamp-light – a scarlet muffler—

(SMITH *starts as if shot.*)

MIGSWORTH (*in a screech*): A what!!!

LANDLORD (*clutching edge of door, mutters*): A scarlet muffler!
(*Slowly* BUTTERS *comes out of a dream.*)

TRAVELLER: Yes. Odd taste, no doubt, but so it was – I say,
what's the matter with your friend? (*Indicates* BUTTERS.)

MIGSWORTH: Kindly excuse him, sir; he's had rather much.

BUTTERS (*muttering*): Hung on a scarlet thread, he was, and
smilin'—

MIGSWORTH (*soothingly*): Come, come, old man!

BUTTERS (*as though not hearing, turns slowly to* TRAVELLER *and extends shaking forefinger*): 'Twas a ghost ye saw this night – the ghost o' Jacob Forge that was hung for murder this mornin' at Lakeford Jail. And he was hung on a thread o' that same scarlet muffler – God rest his soul! (*Relapses into dream.*)

TRAVELLER (*to Migsworth*): I'm afraid all this is beyond me. Incidentally, I should say your friend is not suffering from any over-indulgence, but from some severe mental and nervous strain.

SMITH (*anticipating Migsworth*): 'Tis like enough, sir. William Butters is a good man, and as honest as any grocer could be, in these hard times. Had his difficulties, he had. But he should never ha' gone to see the black flag hoisted this mornin'. Ye see, sir, he had the ill luck to be one o' the jury that sent Jacob Forge, our neighbour, though not our friend, to the gallows, and he's never got over it. Now he's started sayin' to himself: 'What if me and the judge was wrong?'

TRAVELLER (*nodding sympathetically*): And this Jacob Forge – and the scarlet muffler?

SMITH: Why, sir—

MIGSWORTH (*interposing*): In the winter-time Jacob Forge always wore the scarlet muffler – he was well known by it, for there was nothin' like it in Ashley. And on a dark night, on the high road, he murdered an old farmer comin' home from market wi' a bag o' money – near four hundred pounds – beat in his head wi' a hammer, he did!

SMITH: I know that money-bag! Seen it often in my shop.

LANDLORD: Same here! Farmer Jukes never passed my door—

SMITH: And they found the hammer hid in Forge's tool-house wi' blood and a grey hair or two on it. And they found three cheques belongin' to the farmer there also;

but the bag o' notes and cash they never found; he must ha' hid it too safe. And 'twas proved that he was needin' money at the time. We all was, for that matter. Of course at the trial he denied everything; said he was sleepin' in his bed when it happened.

MIGSWORTH: But it was the muffler did for him! Though there was other evidence. He must ha' hid it, too, or burned it, for 'twas never found – he swore he had lost it; thought he had dropped it in one o' the village shops, but couldn't say which—

SMITH: But in the farmer's nails they got a thread of it. The old man would be clawin' at his enemy, ye understand. So 'tis true enough that Jacob Forge was hung on a thread o' scarlet.

LANDLORD (*taking a step forward and clearing his throat*): It should be told, sir, that, even after he was condemned, Forge always believed – or pretended he believed – that something would happen to save him. But (*shaking his head*) the black flag went up, sure enough, this mornin'! I didn't know Forge – he never came here – but I allow it has been a sorrowful day.

(*A clock is heard striking ten.*)

TRAVELLER: Bound to cast a gloom over the place. Was this Forge married?

MIGSWORTH (*getting in first*): No, sir; and he had no friends exceptin' a chap called Breen – another solitudinarian like himself – who has unfortunately been tryin' to drown his grief ever since – as Mr Flett there will confirm.

LANDLORD: Too true, sir, though I do my best to check him. (*Takes out watch; to the three.*) Well, gentlemen, I'm real sorry, but the law must be obeyed.

(MIGSWORTH *empties his tankard.*)

SMITH: Your clock's fast. Considerin' the day it's been and considerin' the night it is – hark to that blast! – Mr Migsworth and me ought to have one more. We'll take it standin' if ye like. (*Empties his tankard.*)

LANDLORD (*holding up watch*): Correct time's here, gentlemen. Sorry, very sorry, indeed!

(*They rise reluctantly.* MIGSWORTH *is about to arouse Butters.*)

TRAVELLER: Perhaps you gentlemen will give me your company for a little longer.

(*They smile delightedly.*)

Right! Two pints, Landlord.

LANDLORD: Very good, sir. If ye'll excuse me, I'll lock up first.

(*Goes out.*)

SMITH: 'Tis too kind.

MIGSWORTH (*in his best manner*): I am deeply obliged.

(*They sit.*)

TRAVELLER: Not at all. But what about your friend?

MIGSWORTH: Best not disturb him, sir. Mr Smith and me will see him home in due season. He should never ha' been on the jury.

TRAVELLER (*lighting fresh cigarette*): What do you two gentlemen think about your friend's ghost theory?

MIGSWORTH: Well, sir, personally, I don't believe in ghosts as a general rule—

SMITH: Nor me – ever!

MIGSWORTH: All the same, I'd swear there's not a livin' man within twenty miles o' Ashley would wear a scarlet muffler now—

SMITH: Hadn't thought o' that. (*Suddenly listening, holds up hand.*) I say, there's somebody comin' in.

(*Disturbance outside; altercation.* LANDLORD's *voice: 'No, no, I can't have it. After ten, you know!'*)

MIGSWORTH: Oh, Lord! I do believe 'tis Breen come back.

TRAVELLER: Breen? – the friend of the murd – the dead man?

MIGSWORTH: Yes, sir; and I'm afraid it means trouble for Flett. Of course Flett *can't* serve him now.

(*Altercation sounds nearer.* BREEN *cursing;* LANDLORD *protesting or trying to soothe.*)

Oh, damn it all, he's comin' in! Hope he won't be unpleasant, sir.

LANDLORD (*outside*): Now, now, Mr Breen, don't ye be unkind. Ye wouldn't like me to lose my licence. It's after hours and if anyone saw ye comin' in— Oh, why didn't I lock the door on the stroke?

BREEN (*outside*): Lemme pass! Fetch a bottle o' whisky. I've got the money. Hear that? All right, fetch it!

LANDLORD: Stop, stop, for the Lord's sake!

(*Sounds of a struggle.*)

Well, well, if I let ye in for a minute, will ye promise not to—? Oh, dear!

(BREEN *enters, flinging the door back on its hinges, followed by dismayed and dishevelled* LANDLORD. *He wears a tarpaulin coat buttoned to the chin and streaming wet. He is hatless. His face is dead white; his eyes fixed and staring. He walks in a steady, mechanical fashion to a chair in the corner, his usual place. Takes no notice of other occupants. Sits.*)

LANDLORD (*halting just inside door, apologetically*): Gentlemen, I couldn't stop him.

TRAVELLER (*under his breath*): Heavens, what a case! (*Beckons* LANDLORD.)

BREEN (*staring at vacancy; in a sing-song voice*): A knife for the silly old judge and a bottle o' whisky for me!

(LANDLORD *comes on tiptoe.*)

TRAVELLER (*whispering*): Whatever happens, not a drop!

LANDLORD: Oh, never! (*Whispering.*) But *is* he – *is* he drunk, sir?

TRAVELLER: Worse! He's on the verge of – never mind. Go back to the door. Wait. Be ready.

BREEN (*without moving*): Poison for the daft jury, and a bottle o' whisky for me!

(*The* TRAVELLER, *gripping the arms of his chair, leans forward, alert, watchful.* SMITH *stares stupidly.* BUTTERS *seems to be coming out of his dream.*)

MIGSWORTH (*with a cough, behind his hand*): What about givin' him some strong coffee, sir?

(TRAVELLER *makes a sign for silence. All is still in the room; but outside the wind rises to a shriek, and a gust of hail strikes the window.*)

BREEN (*as before*): Bottle o' whisky—

(BUTTERS *realizes presence of Breen and sits quietly, gazing. There comes a flash of lightning, a crackle of thunder. All start save* BREEN. *The wind falls with a sob. Silence.*)

BREEN (*as before*): Bottle o' whisky. (*Then his expression changes as though another idea had entered his brain.*) Money! – ye want money—! (*Like an automaton he stands up. The two lowest buttons of the tarpaulin are undone, and drawing aside the skirt he gets at a pocket. Withdraws his fist, stands rigid for a moment or two.*) Money! (*Flings handful of coins on the floor.*) Money! – Whisky!

(*No one stirs.*)

Not enough money? Eh? (*Goes to pocket again. Fetches forth good-sized canvas bag.*) Bottle o' whisky! (*Flings bag with a crash at* LANDLORD's *feet.*) There!

LANDLORD (*recoiling in horror*): Oh, my good God! The farmer's money-bag!

(SMITH, *clutching Migsworth's arm, points at bag.* BUTTERS, *his eyes starting, rises slowly and stands grasping chair-back. His lips move soundlessly.*

BREEN (*his gaze fixed again*): Bottle o'— (*Pause.*) Bottle o'— (*Longer pause.*) Black flag – black flag – black— (*Slowly his mouth opens and shuts like that of gasping fish.*)

(TRAVELLER *rises softly, signalling to Landlord. The gasping stops abruptly, the mouth remaining open.* BREEN *takes two mechanical steps forward.*

The TRAVELLER *slips nearer.* BREEN *rises on his toes.*)

TRAVELLER (*to* LANDLORD): Quick!

(BREEN *pitches forward. The* TRAVELLER *and* LANDLORD *catch him.*)

Here! – in my chair. Get off his coat. (*Undoes coat, throws it open, exposing scarlet muffler round neck and across chest.*) Why, it's the man I nearly—

SMITH (*in a high falsetto*): Oh, oh, oh! – the farmer's money-bag – and the scarlet muffler, too!

(MIGSWORTH *puts his hands to his face.*)

TRAVELLER: Quiet! (*Lays his ear to* BREEN'S *heart – a pause – lifts a grave countenance.*)

(*A silence.* MIGSWORTH *uncovers his face.*)

BUTTERS (*staggers forward, one hand to his head, the other pointing shakily*): Breen, ye damned thief, ye've been burglin' my safe. (*Realizes the significance of his words and stands petrified.*)

(*First the* TRAVELLER, *then* MIGSWORTH, *then* SMITH *and* LANDLORD *recoil from him.*

CURTAIN

PRODUCTION NOTES

This play is essentially a thriller: although we may feel Butter's agony and Breen's torment, the effects are designed to keep up an atmosphere of suspense, death, horror, and mystery, with a build-up to the eventual solution. The first movement would take us up to the Traveller's entry. Within this, the producer would have to bring out the flashes of melodrama accentuating the atmosphere of horror that contrasts with more matter-of-fact moments; against the Landlord's ordinary, courteous words and Migsworth's gossipy tones, there should stand out Butters' emotional outbursts and Smith's deliberate dramatizing: '. . . Oh, my soul!' 'Jacob Forge was hanged by . . . by the neck . . .' Pace should be whipped up to bring out the horror of Forge's execution ('the black flag goin' up . . .') before the flow is held up first by Migsworth's significant question to Butters – why he should have prayed that the black flag might never go up, and then by the Landlord's entry which reduces the tension altogether. In the passage just before the Traveller's entry, two points should be emphasized in production – the Landlord's 'preminotion', and the gradual concentration on Butters, emphasized by noises and lighting effects of the storm and culminating in the high moment of horror expressed in the key words of the title: '. . . hung . . . on a scarlet thread'.

We should be made to feel the relaxation that settles after the Traveller's entry. The storm noises subside; even Butters' muttering about the thread o' scarlet is subdued; and conversation becomes matter of fact. But the pace cannot be allowed to slacken too much: conversation moves smoothly but dramatically to the Traveller's description of how he came upon a man in the middle of the road – a man with a scarlet muffler. The problem in the next sequence is to control Butters's outbursts (dream-like rather than dramatic here) and throw the emphasis on the background story. If the story is told quietly, with restrained drama, the key notes 'thread o' scarlet' and 'black flag' will stand out all the more effectively, and Breen's melodramatic appearance will be the more startling. The last sequence will require careful positioning and timing: lighting should pick out the staggering figure of Breen; and the money-bags and the scarlet muffler must be prominently revealed. The value of a dramatic pause will be strikingly illustrated after the Traveller says 'Quiet'. The producer should concentrate all his effects on the figure of Butters as he approaches, centre stage, the slumped body of Breen. The last words should be dramatically isolated.

TALKING POINTS

On Staging and Acting

1. Consider the sequence up to the second entry of the Landlord. What kinds of characters have been suggested?
   What qualities would you look for in the person cast to
   play Butters? What qualities would you bring out in the
   character of Migsworth?
2. In the sequence that follows, pick out the Landlord's most
   matter-of-fact 'speeches' and his most dramatic 'speeches'.
   Decide the different tones of voice you would use to mark
   the contrast.
3. Work out the relative positions of Migsworth, Butters,
   and Smith, at the entry of the Traveller. Describe the
   movements, mannerisms and gestures that might help to
   establish the personality of the Traveller, and consider also
   what might be his manner of speaking. (Refer to specific
   words, phrases, sentences.)
4. Suggest a plan of the grouping at the entry of Breen and
   the Landlord near the end of the play, and indicate their
   moves up to the moment of the dramatic pause before the
   storm breaks out again. What are the problems of production at this point?
5. What are the final significant moves in the play, and where
   would you place Breen and Butters – and how would you
   group the others – as the curtain comes down? What
   suggestions have you about lighting to emphasize the
   melodrama?

On the Human Situation

1. A thriller has to keep the audience guessing. What false trails does the dramatist lay?
2. This is a *Grand Guignol* type of play. From it what do you think are the general features of *Grand Guignol*?
3. The Traveller is both calm stranger and an intimate part of the action. How does he fulfil both roles?
4. What normal and conventional things underlie and contrast with the abnormal and unconventional elements?
5. Discuss the dramatist's handling of story and dialogue just prior to the final curtain.

Rory Aforesaid

A Comedy in One Act

by

JOHN BRANDANE

John Brandane (1869–1947) was the pen name of Dr John MacIntyre. Born in Bute, as a lad he worked a twelve-hour day in a Glasgow cotton mill, afterwards as a clerk in a warehouse, during which time he studied medicine, qualifying as a doctor in 1901. Settled in Glasgow after World War I, he worked tirelessly at writing plays and encouraging others to write plays for the Scottish National Theatre Society. *Rory Aforesaid* was first staged by the Society in the Lyric Theatre, Glasgow in October 1926, under the direction of Tyrone Guthrie. It is founded on an anonymous fifteenth-century French play which goes under various titles – among them *Maistre Pierre Pathelin*. But John Brandane has so transformed the original that *Rory Aforesaid* can be regarded as a new creation. Its sharp sense of human, and Scottish, absurdities verges at times on farce, yet it manages to keep within the limits of true comedy. The text used here is the one the author wanted to be taken as his final acting version

PERSONS IN THE PLAY

In order of appearance

MACCONNACHIE, *the Court Officer*
DUNCAN MACCALLUM, *merchant and small sheep farmer at Ardnish*
RORY MACCOLL, *shepherd to Mr Maccallum*
MR MCINTOSH, *an Oban lawyer*
THE SHERIFF-SUBSTITUTE, *also from Oban*
MRS MACCLEAN, *a crofter widow-woman*

SCENE: *A court-house in the West Highlands*
TIME: *Twentieth Century*

Applications regarding performances of this play should be addressed to Messrs Curtis Brown Ltd, 13 King Street, Covent Garden, London W.C.2. No performance may be given unless permission has first been obtained.

SET

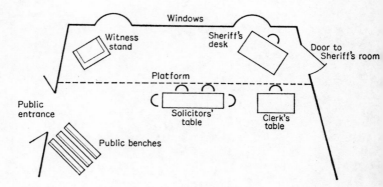

RORY AFORESAID

SCENE: *The Sheriff-Court at Torlochan: a large chamber with whitewashed walls, panelled in lower part with yellow pine. Two tall, gaunt windows are in the back wall. In the left wall, near the back, is a door, leading to the* SHERIFF's *retiring-room. In the right wall, towards the front, is another door, an entrance for the public. To the left is the Sheriff's desk on a low platform; a table for his clerk is at the side of it. In the centre of the floor-space is the table for solicitors, with chairs around it. Between the table and the* SHERIFF'S *desk, but somewhat towards the back, is the witness-stand. To the right are benches for the public.*

DUNCAN MACCALLUM, *merchant and sheep-farmer from Ardnish, is walking up and down the empty chamber to keep himself warm, for there is an October chill in the air. He is an erect old man of sixty, with grizzled hair and beard. He wears a square-topped hat, and a muffler is wound over the collar of his stout overcoat. To him there enters the* COURT OFFICER, *a man of fifty, with his few remaining dark hairs carefully combed in separate lines across the bald portion of his scalp. He wears a black tie, and his square-cut coat has an official look.*

COURT OFFICER: Will you not be coming in to the fire in the waiting-room, Mr MacCallum? It's cold in this big tomb of a place.

MACCALLUM: No, no! I'm fine here. I want to get used to the Court, you see. I'm forty miles from home, you understand, and I just feel like a fish out of water.

COURT OFFICER: Ach, don't be exciting yourself, now.

MACCALLUM (*looking at a yellow paper in his hand*): What a lot of 'saids' and 'aforesaids' they put into a summons!

COURT OFFICER: Well, that's the law, you see. When a lawyer's making a speech he feels fine if he says 'aforesaid,' every now and again.

MACCALLUM: Do you tell me now? I never thought of that! (*He reads.*) 'The sheep aforesaid' – yes, yes – you'd think it was a very special sheep, if you said it that way. I wonder now if I could be trying that myself when I'm giving my evidence. 'Rory MacColl aforesaid.' That's fine!

COURT OFFICER: Ach, now, don't you be trying any of that nonsense!

MACCALLUM: Well, I'll just be going over in my own mind what I'll be saying to the Sheriff; and then I'll feel more at home when he comes in, you understand. This will be the witness-box?

(*He crosses to the witness-stand.*)

COURT OFFICER: It is that.

MACCALLUM: There would be no harm in my standing in it for a wee minute, just to accustom myself to the way I would be feeling when my turn comes?

COURT OFFICER: No harm at all, Mr MacCallum! Go you in and welcome!

MACCALLUM: Och, you're very kind – very kind – indeed, yes. (*He goes to the witness-stand, and holds up his right hand, mumbling over the words of the oath to himself, then smiles, bows and steps down.*) Yes, yes, I'll be doing fine. All the same I'd feel easier if my lawyer was with me this day.

COURT OFFICER: And have you no lawyer then for this case?

MACCALLUM: Well, I was to have had Mr Thomson from the Oban – the young one – the good one; but the ten o'clock steamer could not take the pier this morning because of the high wind; and the poor man will have been carried on to Mallaig most likely. It's a good thing I came myself by last night's steamer.

COURT OFFICER: It's a peety for Mr Thomson being taken so far out of his way.

MACCALLUM: Och, well, it's a lawyer's fee saved. And I'll do as well as any lawyer when it comes to the bit.

COURT OFFICER: All the same I like to see a man with his lawyer when a Court is held.

MACCALLUM: But, man, man! What need of a lawyer when I saw Rory kill the sheep with my own eyes? A fine sheep it was, too – as fine a gimmer as ever you saw, Mr MacConnachie.

COURT OFFICER: So I was hearing; but you're forty miles away as you say, and we didna hear much of the business at this end of the country.

(*The door opens, and* RORY MACCOLL *comes in. He is a Highland shepherd, aged sixty, and carries a cromag, or long crook of hazel. His bearded face is old and weathered, as is also his suit of rough homespun. His eyes are sharp and twinkling. At sight of him* MACCALLUM *turns away in disgust.*)

RORY: A fine day, Mr MacCallum.

(MACCALLUM *does not reply.* RORY *looks up and round the Court-house inquiringly. The* COURT OFFICER *goes towards him.*)

COURT OFFICER: Good day! Are you in this case?

RORY: I am that. It's a great stack of stones, this Court-house. What time will you be wanting me?

(*He hands some yellow papers to the Court Officer.*)

COURT OFFICER (*reading them*): Ach! it's you, it is? – Rory MacColl. Eleven o'clock. You'll be having half an hour to wait.

RORY: Half an hour! Is there an Inns in this place?

COURT OFFICER: There is that. But if I were you, I'd not go

near the Inns till your case is over. There's a fire in the waiting-room out there.

RORY: But they'll have a fire in the Inns, too?

COURT OFFICER: I'm thinking the waiting-room fire will be safer for the like of you, Rory.

RORY (*grinning, as he goes out easily*): Well, I could be taking a look at both of them, surely.

MACCALLUM (*fuming*): Did you hear that? The cheek of him! Killing my sheep, and then wishing me a good day, as cool as you like!

COURT OFFICER: So that's the man, is it? What way did you not have the police take him up on a criminal charge?

MACCALLUM: 'Deed and I don't know why the police would not do that same, when I asked them. They just said there was too much sheep's-head broth in it, and advised me to claim for damages.

COURT OFFICER: Only a small debt case, is it? Well, well!

MACCALLUM: Aye, just that. But wait you, and see if it will not turn out a perjury case, before we're done with it. Wait till you hear Rory swearing away his soul this day! You never heard his like for the great flow of language. English or Gaelic, it's all the same to Rory – there's no stopping the lying tongue of him!

COURT OFFICER: As bad as that!

MACCALLUM: Aye, as bad as that! Wait you! For if this place is not struck by lightning as soon as Rory opens his dirty mouth, my name is not Duncan MacCallum.

COURT OFFICER: Ach, if it's lies brings down the lightning, this place would have been rock and lime long ago.

MACCALLUM: Well, well! And is that the way of it?

(MR MACINTOSH, *a lawyer from Oban, enters, carrying a black gown on his arm. He is a man of fifty, clean-shaven, and bald-headed. He has narrow, quizzing eyes.*)

COURT OFFICER: Good day, Mr MacIntosh.

MACINTOSH: Oh, good day, Mr MacConnachie. Look here, this isn't the gown I left here a week ago.

COURT OFFICER: I'm sorry, Mr MacIntosh. Some of the other lawyers must have taken yours last Tuesday. Just you be doing with that one for the present.

MACINTOSH: It's a confounded nuisance, you know.
(*He turns to go out.*)

MACCALLUM (*coming forward*): Good day to you, sir!

MACINTOSH: Oh, good day! I'm afraid I haven't the pleasure of knowing you.

COURT OFFICER: This is the pursuer, sir – Mr MacCallum of Ardnish.

MACCALLUM: Yes, yes. Now isn't it strange that you'll not remember me? You got some Harris tweed out of my shop at Ardnish, a year ago last August.

MACINTOSH: Ardnish? I was never in Ardnish all my life, I'm sorry to say. But a fine place, I hear.

MACCALLUM: Och, yes, but you *were* in Ardnish. Yes, yes – a year ago last August. And I mistook you for a Mr Mac-Farlane, a great salmon-fisher that was staying at Ardnish Hotel.

MACINTOSH: Well, I'm no salmon-fisher, Mr MacCallum. And I was never in Ardnish at any time. You're mistaken.

MACCALLUM: Am I saying you are a salmon-fisher? . . . All I'm saying is that there were many strangers about that day, and you were one of them. And the name you had then was not MacIntosh, but MacFarlane.

MACINTOSH: Sir, do you doubt my word? I tell you again I was never in Ardnish in all my life!

MACCALLUM: Och, yes, but you were. A year ago last August. And off you went just in time to catch the steamer. And that tweed was never paid for. And me not seeing you from that day to this.

MACINTOSH: Is this a joke, sir?

MACCALLUM: No joke about it. Never a penny did I get from you.

MACINTOSH: I tell you, sir, it must have been somebody else.

MACCALLUM: And I tell you I never forget a face or a voice. And what I say to you is: Pay me for the tweed you stole away from me a year ago last August.

MACINTOSH: Stole? – stole? You hear what this man says, MacConnachie? (*He takes out paper and pencil, and makes a note hurriedly.*) He accuses me of theft, and I take you as a witness.

COURT OFFICER: Ach, no, no! I've enough to do with putting other people into the witness-box, let alone myself! For goodness' sake, be settling it among yourselves!

MACINTOSH: But this is too serious a matter to pass over, Mr MacConnachie. Excuse me a moment. (*He goes to the door at back, and calls.*) Mr MacColl! (RORY *enters.*) This isn't your case yet, Mr MacColl. But something almost as important. (MACCALLUM *moves away, but* MACINTOSH *puts a hand on his arm.*) Just a moment, sir. Will you now have the kindness to repeat before this good man the words you have just used about myself?

MACCALLUM: Good man? And who are you calling a good man? (*Then to* RORY.) Well, you may be a good man, as Neil of the Mountain said to the cat, but you haven't the face of one.

RORY: And who are you to be talking? You're nothing but a whistle and a noise, when all's said and done. Man, man! you'd make a stirk laugh.

MACINTOSH: Never mind, Mr MacColl. Just let him repeat what he said a moment ago in the presence of Mr MacConnachie here.

MACCALLUM: 'Deed, and I'll do nothing so foolish. But I'll be seeing my lawyer tomorrow, about you and my Harris tweed.

MACINTOSH: What Harris tweed?

MACCALLUM: The Harris tweed you stole from me a year ago last August.

MACINTOSH: Ah! I thought that would fetch you. You heard, Rory? He said 'stole'.

RORY: He did that.

MACCALLUM: Och, I'll be staying here no longer with such a pair of thieves.

RORY: Well, it's a poor pair that's no match for one.
(MACCALLUM *flounces out, shouting.*)

MACCALLUM: I said thieves and I'll stick to it, look you!

MACINTOSH: You observe, Rory? He said 'thieves'. You heard, MacConnachie. Please take a note, both of you.
(*He scribbles industriously himself.*)

COURT OFFICER: Ach, I'm not taking any notes. I've my own work to attend to.
(*He goes out angrily.*)

MACINTOSH (*still scribbling*): All right. Please take a note, Rory, that Mr MacConnachie refuses to take a note.

RORY: Och, no need for notes, for I'll be minding all he said. And I'm no scholar with the pen, anyway.

MACINTOSH (*shutting his notebook with a snap, angrily*): The idea! Why, I never was in Ardnish in all my life! Called me a thief, did he? Well, he'll find it's not one penny will settle this little business!

RORY: Yes, yes! But about my own case, now? You were saying you would be giving me the good advice before the Court started.

MACINTOSH: It's awkward doing that here. Somebody might come in. And we've lost time, too, with that fool. (*He makes for the door, but turns.*) No, we can't go into the witness-room now. Tell you what. Put your foot against that door. (RORY *does so.*) Thank you. And now I'll give you a few hints. (*He paces up and down, cogitating.*) The old ruffian! Called me a thief! Well, we'll see. Tuts! Him and his Harris tweed!

RORY: I wish you'd leave that Harris tweed alone, and tell me what to say about the sheep I killed.

MACINTOSH: Aha! So you did kill it? Last Tuesday you told me that you didn't kill it!

RORY: Yes, yes; I told you that.

MACINTOSH: Well, will you go into that box today and swear on oath that you did not kill it?

RORY: Look you! Some of them poor sheep are that bad with the braxy they're far better killed.

MACINTOSH: I know all that. But will you take your oath that you did not kill MacCallum's sheep?

RORY: Och, take an oath, is it?

MACINTOSH: Yes.

RORY: No, no! I have my religion; and I'll take no oath.

MACINTOSH: You say you did not kill this sheep?

RORY (*hesitatingly*): No.

MACINTOSH: Then why not swear as before Almighty God that you didn't?

RORY: Och, no! I have my religion, you'll understand. I'm not liking that oath at all, at all.

MACINTOSH: Well, what are you going to tell the Sheriff?

RORY: I'll tell him MacCallum didn't see me kill the sheep.

MACINTOSH: But MacCallum will swear that he did see you.

RORY: Och, no, it was too dark that night. He couldna see me.

MACINTOSH: Man alive! You'll lose your case, if you say that! Look here, Rory! Unless you promise to take the oath, and say you didn't kill that sheep, I'll fling up your case.

RORY: Now, now, Mr MacIntosh, be you a good man! Don't you be angry with poor Rory. See you this! (*He turns out a dirty purse.*) Look at the good pound notes I have for paying you – that is, if I'll win the case.

MACINTOSH: My good fellow, you must pay me, I'm afraid, whether you win or lose.

RORY: Och, is it pay you, if I lose? No, no!

MACINTOSH: Look here, you old humbug! I've had enough of this. You must promise me here and now to settle up as soon as the case is finished. Otherwise, I'm off home with the one o'clock steamer.

RORY: Och, very well! The man that divides the pudding will have the thick end to himself, I can see! But I'll promise, if there are to be no oaths.

MACINTOSH: You are a stubborn old mule. Why! the Sheriff won't hear you, unless you take the oath.

RORY: I could be having a sore throat, look you, and no can speak.

MACINTOSH: Good! But no – that won't do. He'd ask you to nod your head very likely as he repeated the oath to you. Tell you what, though! Say something silly every time he addresses you, or when anyone speaks to you at all. Understand?

RORY (*parrot fashion*): 'Something silly.'

MACINTOSH: You are an ass! Aha! I've got it. You're not an ass, Rory, you're a sheep!

RORY: Is it me – a sheep?

MACKINTOSH: Yes, a sheep. And every time you're spoken to by way of question you must answer like a sheep. Like this – *Meh!* Understand?

RORY: *Meh!*

MACINTOSH: Splendid. The Sheriff will think you're off your head, and ask you to stand down. Besides, since MacCallum has no lawyer with him he's sure to mix his case all up. We're in luck, old son, we're in luck! Ha-ha!

RORY: Aye, laugh away! But it may be no laughing for me, if the Sheriff gets cross. Man, man! if I had a boil, and you squeezing it, you'd still be laughing.

MACINTOSH: Sorry, Rory! No offence! But, tell me, who is MacCallum's agent? It's quite true, isn't it, that he was carried past the pier in the ten o'clock steamer?

RORY: Yes, it's true enough. It was Mr Thomson from the Oban.

MACINTOSH: Well, he can't get back today, anyway. Good thing I took the eight o'clock boat, or where would you have been, eh?

RORY: *Meh!*

MACINTOSH: Splendid! You'll look as daft as Lachie Gorra! And MacCallum will be no better when I've finished cross-examining him, let me tell you. Besides, the Sheriff will be in a hurry. He always expects a round of golf before lunch on a Tuesday, if I know his little ways. You watch him scuttling off, as soon's we're through. Fine! Fine! (*He rubs his hands. There is a sound of voices outside the door at right.*) Hush! They're coming! Quick! Take your foot away from that door now.

(*They both come forward into the body of the Courthouse.*)

COURT OFFICER (*entering with* MACCALLUM): Will you please sit here, Mr MacCallum? (*He indicates table.*)

MACCALLUM: Thank you, Mr MacConnachie.

(*He sits down at table, and, drawing out his notes, cons them carefully.* MACINTOSH *takes a seat at the opposite end of the table, and refers to his papers also.*)

COURT OFFICER (*to* RORY): You'll sit here, Rory. (*He indicates the front bench, facing the Sheriff's desk.*)

RORY: *Meh!*

COURT OFFICER: What did you say?

RORY: *Meh!*

(MACCALLUM *looks up in astonishment. Some of the* CROFTERS *and* TOWNSFOLK *who have entered titter, as they take their seats in the back benches. The* COURT OFFICER *goes out, and ushers in the* SHERIFF, *bewigged and gowned.*)

COURT OFFICER: Court!

(ALL *stand, and after the* SHERIFF *has taken his seat, sit again. The* COURT OFFICER *whispers to the Sheriff, pointing to MacCallum. The* SHERIFF *puts his hand to his ear, and says: 'Eh?' The* COURT OFFICER *whispers more loudly. It is evident that his lordship is slightly deaf: and from the way he peers at his papers it is also clear that he doesn't see very well. Throughout the trial his deafness and defective vision are clearly indicated by his various gestures. At times he does not make out who is addressing whom.*)

SHERIFF: Ah, most unfortunate! I'm sorry, Mr MacCallum, to hear that your solicitor has been carried past the pier, because of the storm this morning. That is so, isn't it?

MACCALLUM: Yes, my lord.

SHERIFF: Then I suppose you will put forward your own case?

MACCALLUM: If you please, my lord.

SHERIFF: Very well. Go on.

(MACCALLUM *nods to the* COURT OFFICER, *who goes out by door at back.*)

COURT OFFICER (*in a loud voice*): Mrs MacLean!

(MRS MACLEAN, *a stout Highland crofter-woman, with a shock of red hair, appears. She is flustered, and has an aggressive air, as she is ushered into the witness-box.*)

SHERIFF: You are Mrs MacLean, Ardnish?

MRS MACLEAN: Yes, my lord.

SHERIFF (*holding up right hand*): 'I swear by Almighty God.'

MRS MACLEAN (*holding up right hand*): 'I swear by Almighty God.'

SHERIFF: 'As I shall answer to God.'

MRS MACLEAN: 'As I shall answer to God.'

SHERIFF: 'At the great day of judgment.'

MRS MACLEAN: 'At the great day of judgment.'

SHERIFF: 'That I will tell the truth.'

MRS MACLEAN: 'That I will tell the truth.'

SHERIFF: 'The whole truth.'

MRS MACLEAN: 'The whole truth.'

SHERIFF: 'And nothing but the truth.'

MRS MACLEAN: 'And nothing but the truth.'

MACCALLUM (*rising and turning over his papers excitedly*):
Mrs MacLean, was you very fond of sheep's-head broth?

MRS MACLEAN: I was that.

SHERIFF: Louder, please. I can't hear.

MRS MACLEAN: I – was – that.

SHERIFF: Thank you.

MACCALLUM: Was it known to the defender, the aforesaid
Rory MacColl, that you was very fond of sheep's-head
broth?

MRS MACLEAN: It was that.

MACCALLUM: Did he ask yourself and Widow MacIver to a
meal of sheep's-head broth on the day of the 28th March
last?

MRS MACLEAN: Was that a Thursday?

MACCALLUM: It was that.

SHERIFF: A little louder, please. What did you say, Mr
MacCallum?

MACCALLUM: I said, 'It was that,' O lord – I mean, *my* lord.

SHERIFF: Thank you! Go on, Mrs MacLean. Tell us if that
Thursday was the 28th of March.

MRS MACLEAN: Och, I'll no' can mind. But it was the day
after Rory killed the sheep.

SHERIFF: Stop! – stop! – stop! You really must not say a thing
like that. It has not yet been proved that anybody killed a
sheep. Answer the question – no more. You mean that it
was on the day after Mr MacCallum's sheep was said to be
killed?

MRS MACLEAN: Said to be killed? It was killed. How else
could we have the sheep's-head broth?

SHERIFF: But you must not say that. Just answer my question.

MRS MACLEAN: And where could Rory have got a sheep's-head but from a sheep?

SHERIFF: Ahem! I am afraid, Mr MacCallum, I am trespassing on your field, but with your permission, I'll interrogate this witness myself.

(MACCALLUM *bows and sits down.*)

MACCALLUM: Certainly, O lord.

SHERIFF: Now, Mrs MacLean! You had a meal of sheep's-head broth with Rory MacColl on Thursday, the 28th day of March last? Is that so?

MRS MACLEAN: It was a Thursday, anyway.

SHERIFF: But is there nothing you can remember which happened about that time that will help you to the exact date?

MRS MACLEAN: Well, I saw Rory having the sheep's-head singed at the smiddy on the morning of the day we had the sheep's-head broth.

SHERIFF: Well, what morning was that?

MRS MACLEAN: The morning after the night that Rory killed the sheep.

SHERIFF (*more in sorrow than in anger*): That will do, Mrs MacLean. Any questions, Mr MacIntosh?

MACINTOSH: No, my lord.

SHERIFF: Stand down, Mrs MacLean.

(*The* COURT OFFICER *leads the bewildered* MRS MACLEAN *out of the room.* MACCALLUM *leaves the table and enters the witness-box. He takes the oath in the same way as the former witness.*)

SHERIFF: Well, tell us your story, Mr MacCallum.

MACCALLUM: My lord, having lost of late half a score of sheep, without having had from the aforesaid Rory Mac-Coll a satisfactory account of their decease—

SHERIFF: Did you say 'disease'?

MACCALLUM: Any way you like it, my lord. They were

dead, anyway, my lord – or as good as dead, for I never saw them after the first dipping.

SHERIFF: Yes, yes. Go on, please. Time is short, Mr Mac-Callum. Never mind about the dipping.

MACCALLUM: I decided therefore to watch said defender, having suspected the deceased Rory – the aforesaid Rory – of having caused decease of sheep aforesaid.

(MACINTOSH *laughs audibly behind his hand, hanging his head.* MACCALLUM *hears him, and says angrily*):

Aye, laugh away, MacIntosh! But I'm not forgetting that Harris tweed.

SHERIFF (*not perceiving the cause of the interruption*): What's this? We don't want anything irrelevant. Please let us keep to our sheep.

MACCALLUM: Yes. my lord. And a fine sheep it was – as fine a gimmer as ever you saw. I watched Rory through a hole in the wall of the fank on the night of the 27th March last, and saw him kill the sheep – the said 27th of March being the night before the beforesaid sheep's-head broth was made by Rory aforesaid. (MACINTOSH *laughs again involuntarily.*) Aye, laugh away, Mr MacIntosh, but I'll be even with you yet!

SHERIFF: What's that? Whatever are you talking about, sir?

MACCALLUM: I'm talking about the good Harris tweed that was stole from me, and never paid for, O lord!

SHERIFF: I really can't follow you, Mr MacCallum. Let us come back to our sheep, if you please.

MACCALLUM: Very good, my lord. I saw Rory aforesaid cut off the head of my good gimmer before my very eyes, meaning said head, no doubt, for the sheep's-head broth to be made on the 28th March aforesaid. (MACINTOSH *laughs again.*) Yes, you may laugh! But all the same I'll make you pay for the ten yards of tweed you took away in your trap.

SHERIFF: Ten yards in a trap? Whatever are you saying now, Mr MacCallum? Whoever heard of ten yards of a sheep?

MACCALLUM: No, my lord. Ten yards of good Harris tweed. Crotal colour it was. And it never paid for, since a year ago last August.

SHERIFF: I really don't follow you. Do, please, let us get back to our sheep. I really wish you had a legal representative here, Mr MacCallum. Continue.

MACCALLUM: I saw him kill the sheep by cutting its throat first of all, my lord. And then, thinking maybe of the afore-said sheep's-head broth, he cut off the sheeps'-head to make the broth aforesaid. (MACINTOSH *chuckles once more*.) Look at him laughing. But you did not laugh when you got into your trap and drove off with the tweed you never paid for?

SHERIFF: Do I understand you to say that the defender caught the sheep in a trap? Was it a variety of sheep known as a Harris sheep? I thought that breed was extinct.

MACCALLUM: My lord, it wasn't the sheep that was in the trap. It was the tweed – good Harris tweed, and crotal at that.

SHERIFF: Ah! You mean that the wool lost by the disappear-ance of the sheep was equivalent to so much good Harris tweed? Is that it? If that is so, never mind about the tweed just now. We are not concerned with the possible products of the sheep.

MACCALLUM: Well, if your lordship will allow me to say so, I'm really more concerned about the tweed than the sheep.

SHERIFF: Yes, yes, I know. But the sheep comes first, then the wool, then the spinning and the dyeing, then the weaving of the tweed. I know all that. But the sheep comes before the tweed, doesn't it?

MACCALLUM: Well, in this case it didn't, my lord. The tweed was stolen long before the sheep was killed. It was a year ago last August.

SHERIFF: Ahem! I am afraid I must ask you to discontinue, Mr MacCallum. Time is short; and I can't follow you into all these irrelevancies. . . . Now, Mr MacIntosh.

MACINTOSH: Mr MacCallum, you say you saw the defender kill the sheep on the night of the 27th March last?

MACCALLUM: I did that.

MACINTOSH: At what o'clock did you see this?

MACCALLUM: About nine o'clock.

MACINTOSH: Was there a moon that night?

MACCALLUM: No.

MACINTOSH: Had defender a light in the fank?

MACCALLUM: No.

MACINTOSH: What kind of knife had he?

MACCALLUM: I did not see the knife.

MACINTOSH: You did not see the knife? Why?

MACCALLUM: It was too dark.

MACINTOSH: So that you could not see the knife; and yet you saw him kill the sheep?

MACCALLUM: I heard him swearing at the sheep, and saying he'd soon kill it. And then I heard the poor beast struggling and groaning, and then it stopped all at once.

MACINTOSH: Ah! So you did not really *see* him kill the sheep? You heard him kill the sheep?

MACCALLUM: Yes. I heard him kill the sheep.

MACINTOSH: You heard some sounds, and you thought those sounds came from a sheep in process of being killed?

MACCALLUM: I heard him kill the sheep.

MACINTOSH: I understand. You admit, then, that you did not see him kill the sheep?

MACCALLUM: I heard him kill the sheep.

MACINTOSH: Very well. Now, Mr MacCallum, attend to me! Will you please tell his lordship if it is not the case that a sheep struggles and groans if someone gives it a dose of medicine?

MACCALLUM: It might well do that.

MACINTOSH: So that the struggling and groaning you heard might not have been the sounds of a sheep in process of being killed.

MACCALLUM: I heard him kill the sheep.

MACINTOSH: Very well. Now, will you please explain to his lordship what you mean when you say that you saw the defendant with a sheep of the species called Harris, and measuring ten yards; the said sheep being caught in a trap?

MACCALLUM: Never you mind what I mean, Mr MacIntosh, or Mr MacFarlane or whatever your name is! . . . But I say you stole a roll of Harris tweed from me in Ardnish, a year ago last August; and it's never paid for yet!

MACINTOSH (*sitting down*): Thank you.

SHERIFF: That will do, Mr MacCallum. Stand down.

(MACCALLUM, *fuming, is led back to his seat at the table by the Court Officer.* RORY *is then taken to the witness-box, at a sign from* MACINTOSH.)

COURT OFFICER: You're next, Rory.

MACINTOSH: His name is Rory MacColl, my lord – the defender, aged sixty-two. He hasn't much English.

SHERIFF (*writing*): Very good. (*Then, holding up his right hand.*) 'I swear by Almighty God.' (RORY *is silent.*) Repeat after me. 'I swear—' He has some English, hasn't he, Mr Mac-Intosh?

MACINTOSH: Oh, yes, my lord.

SHERIFF: Can you hear me?

RORY: *Meh!*

SHERIFF: What do you say?

RORY: *Meh!*

SHERIFF: I beg pardon. Again?

RORY: *Meh!*

SHERIFF: Is this man *compos mentis*, Mr MacIntosh?

MACINTOSH: He has certainly been very queer of late, my

lord. Indeed, ever since this dreadful charge has been levelled
against him he has been odd in his manner. He has always
been of a gentle, trustful nature. And now that he finds the
harsh realities of the world quite other than he had dreamt
them to be, it may quite well have fallen out that his mind
has become unhinged.

SHERIFF: My dear sir, if there are many more witnesses in this
case like this man and his two predecessors, my own mind
will certainly become unhinged. See what you can make of
him; and then I'll sum up the case.

MACINTOSH: Thank you, my lord. Now attend to me
Mr MacColl. Did you ever at any time or under any circumstances kill a sheep belonging to Mr MacCallum?

RORY: *Meh!*

MACINTOSH: Answer me properly, please. Where did you
get the sheep's-head, of which you made a broth?

RORY: *Meh!*

MACINTOSH: Can't you understand what I say?

RORY: *Meh!*

MACINTOSH (*to the Sheriff, who is listening intently, with his
hand at his ear*): I am afraid it's no use, my lord. The poor
man's head has been turned by this ordeal.

SHERIFF (*dryly*): Yes. Just so. I am afraid, Mr MacIntosh, you
also are of a gentle, trustful disposition. This man may be as
you say, yet other explanations are possible. But time
is short; and we need not go into that. The defender is
evidently – evidently, I say, unable to give us any help. The
pursuer's case rests on that of Mrs MacLean and himself.
The fact that Mrs MacLean supped off sheep's-head broth
along with the defender on a date of great uncertainty is no
doubt of interest, but it is irrelevant. And the pursuer's
evidence is also unsatisfactory. He did not see defender kill
the sheep. He only heard some sounds, which he interpreted
as those emitted by a sheep in its death-agony. I am not an

authority on the sounds emitted by sheep, although after listening to Mr MacColl's performance in the witness-box, I feel as if, with a little further study, I might qualify as such. But one does not require to be such an authority to see that Mr MacCallum may have misinterpreted the sounds he heard. I express my regret that Mr MacCallum's solicitor was not here to help him with his case. Judgment for the defender, with expenses.

(*He rises to go, and all stand as he retires. The* COURT OFFICER *follows; and the* PEOPLE *crowd round Rory, congratulating him.* RORY *only grins and returns numerous handshakes without uttering a word.* MACCALLUM *strides over to MacIntosh.*)

MACCALLUM: You'll hear more about that tweed before very long, my hero.

(*But* MACINTOSH *only sniggers happily as he makes out an account for Rory; and* MACCALLUM *goes off, furious.* MACINTOSH *rises with his bill, and interrupts the rejoicings over Rory's victory.*)

MACINTOSH: Here you are, Rory. It should be five guineas, but we'll say five pounds. (*He hands Rory the bill.*)

RORY (*regarding the bill and then* MACINTOSH's *extended hand*): *Meh!*

MACINTOSH: Come on, you old rascal! Five pounds.

RORY: *Meh-h-h!*

CURTAIN

GLOSSARY

braxy: diseased sheep
crotal: reddish-brown
fank: sheep pen

gimmer: young sheep
stirk: bullock

PRODUCTION NOTES

Part of the comic effect of this play lies in the contrast between the simplicity and homeliness of characters like Rory Mac-Callum and Mrs MacLean on the one hand, and the formality of the court setting and legal procedure on the other. Above all, stage production should aim at showing how Rory's personality and intelligence triumph over all the attempts to control and defeat him.

The first touch of comedy to be marked would be Mac-Callum's childish delight in using the word 'aforesaid', and the phrase 'Rory MacColl aforesaid' should be rolled on the tongue as a theme in music. The second important comic touch comes when Rory and MacCallum meet for the first time in the courthouse: MacCallum's annoyance must be clearly evident, perhaps even overacted; while Rory's cheerfulness and self-assurance must be firmly established. In the meeting of MacCallum and MacIntosh, the important thing is to emphasize the vigour and irrelevance of the quarrel about the tweed MacIntosh is accused of stealing. The comedy lies in the way each man in turn loses his temper about something completely irrelevant – MacCallum because of this imagined 'theft' and MacIntosh because of the 'unjustified' accusation. Producers should encourage over-acting here to stress the absurdity.

If the solemnity of the opening court procedure is stressed, Mrs MacLean's interrogation will be all the funnier. Her homely, comically logical replies must be made promptly to the Sheriff's official questions; and it might help if the Sheriff tends to overact and underspeak. The first part of

MacCallum's interrogation is long-winded and confused: the comedy lies in his pompous use of the word 'aforesaid' and in his mixing up the alleged theft of the tweed and the stealing of the sheep. The second part is brisk and sharp: MacIntosh deliberately leads MacCallum to make statements that damage his case. This passage must be paced up briskly.

The final interrogation – Rory's – is in two parts; and in both, as Rory answers 'Meh', there should be a strong suggestion of farce in the playing. Both MacIntosh and the Sheriff reintroduce the formal legal note that steadies the play and announces Rory's success; but the farce should return at the end. Players and producer should not be afraid to let the play dissolve into a romp.

TALKING POINTS

On Staging and Acting

1. Plan the grouping at Rory's first entrance. Where would you place MacCallum to emphasize his annoyance and dislike of Rory; and where and how would you stage the short dialogue between Rory and the Court Officer? What suggestions would you make to your actors about their style of walking and speaking?

2. How would you group and stage the quarrel between Mac-Callum and MacIntosh, and at what point would you whip up the pace of the speaking? Remember that the Court Officer and (later) Rory are also on the stage during this scene.

3. What comic touches would you introduce in the conspiracy scene in which it is decided that Rory should act a sheep?

4. Describe how you would organize, group and direct the big scene of the entry of the public and the entry of the Sheriff. Remember the importance of the exact placing of characters on the stage and the importance of the timing of the entries.

5. Consider the conclusion of the play and write instructions for the players to help them to bring out what you think are the comic touches most likely to appeal to the audience.

On the Human Situation

1. David and the Goliaths.
2. The dramatist develops the idea that human beings

sometimes distort their own natures, with consequent contortions. Discuss.

3. The Sheriff Substitute acts according to the strict laws of evidence. In what ways then does the law become 'an ass'?

4. How, for comic purposes, does the dramatist manipulate (a) what the characters know of the play (b) what the audience knows?

5. Who tries to cheat whom and what kinds of amusement result?

The Pardoner's Tale

A Morality in One Act
adapted from Geoffrey Chaucer

by

JAMES BRIDIE

James Bridie (1888–1951) was the pen-name of Dr Osborne Henry Mavor, who was educated at Glasgow Academy and Glasgow University, graduating as a doctor in 1913. Persuaded by John Brandane to read plays submitted by others to the Scottish National Theatre Society, he soon turned to writing his own; the first under the pen-name of Mary Henderson and produced by Tyrone Guthrie. He is now established as one of the major dramatists of Scotland. *The Pardoner's Tale*, developed from a tale of Chaucer, was written in 1930. In it he displays his ability to concentrate much into small space, his inventiveness of phrase, his discrimination of characters, and that penetrating and devastating moral sense that was one of the hallmarks of his greater full-length plays. *The Pardoner's Tale*, brief though it is, reminds us of that other morality play, more elaborate and more subtle, by Sir David Lindsay, *Ane Pleasant Satire of the Thrie Estatis*.

PERSONS IN THE PLAY

In order of appearance

AN OLD INNKEEPER

DUNCAN ELLIOT ⎫
HANDASYDE GRANT ⎬ *Three second-rate bucks from Edinburgh*
PHILIP MACGILLIVRAY ⎭

SCENE: *A changehouse on the Perth Road, Night.*
TIME: *Early Eighteenth Century*

Applications regarding performances of this play should be addressed to Messrs Curtis Brown Ltd, 13 King Street, Covent Garden, London W.C.2. No performance may be given unless permission has first been obtained.

SET

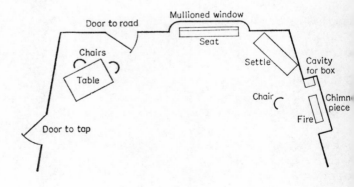

THE PARDONER'S TALE

*The scene is a dilapidated changehouse between Edinburgh and
Perth. The time is early in the eighteenth century. It is winter.
The room has two doors: one at the back opening on the road and
another, right, leading to the tap. The wainscoting has fallen
from the bare walls years ago; and the furniture is a table, a
window-seat below a mullioned window, some of whose panes
have been broken and stuffed with rags, and two or three rickety
chairs of different periods. There is a fine chimney-piece in bad
repair, and in front of a poor log fire there sits an old man
thinking. The room is lit by a storm lantern, but candles are
standing ready.*
*The old man gets up, pulls a green log from under the window-seat,
and mends the fire. As he does so, the noise of beating on the
door is heard. He opens the door, after lighting his candles, and*
THREE HORSEMEN *with snow on their cloaks fall out of the
darkness.*

FIRST HORSEMAN: Cock's body, it's cold. St Judas Iscariot,
what a house you keep! Where's the ostler?

OLD MAN: I am ostler and chambermaid and host in this house
these two years, sir.

FIRST HORSEMAN: Hell's guts, and do you tell me that? Blast
my eyes, on a nicht that would freeze the liver out of Beel-
zebub to stumble on a damned charnel-house the like of
this! See the horses stabled, then, and back with you like the
hammers of hell with a stoup of aqua-vitae. Run, or I'll
cut the spine out of ye!

OLD MAN: Speedily, sir, speedily.

(*He goes out. The* FIRST HORSEMAN *flings off his cloak. The* SECOND RIDER *reels to the fireside and sits down. The* THIRD *sits on the window-seat and buries his head in his hands. All three horsemen are dressed like gentlemen. The first two are brieflless advocates, the third a student. The first is a big red-headed fellow, Duncan Elliot, a bully, the soberest but noisiest of the party. The second Handasyde Grant, is a little blackavised man, all tipsy ingratiatingness but with a cur's bite below his cringing. The third, Philip Macgillivray, is the only decent-looking fellow of the lot — a debauched Galahad, fairheaded, with a Highland accent and the remnants of a Highland gentility. He is sick and nearly exhausted. Elliot sings in a loud brutal voice, beating time on the table with his riding-crop.*)

ELLIOT: 'It's Geordie he sat down to dine,
And wha came in but Madame Swine;
Grump, grump, quo' she, I'm come in time,
I'll sit and dine wi' Geordie!
The sow's tail is till him yet,
The sow's birse will kill him yet . . .'

GRANT: In the name of God, man! Stop. Stop. Stop. Do you want us all hangit?

ELLIOT: Hangit, by Satan! . . . 'The sow's tail is till him yet . . .'

GRANT: Now, Mr Elliot. Now, Dunny, now. Now, now now. There's songs that's decent among gentlemen, and there's songs that give offence, in a way of speaking, if ye see what I mean. You ken I'm a loyal subject. And I ken you're a loyal subject. And Philip's loyal subject, too. All loyal subjects King Geordie. Now, I say nothing against you. You're my friend. Very well then, you say nothing against Geordie. That's fair speaking. Forbye you're making the poor young doctor sick.

ELLIOT: Cock's body, I forgot about him. How is it with you my poor wee yaud?

PHILIP: Let me alone.

GRANT: Let me alone! There's a hearty good fellow for you! There's the life and soul of the festive round! Whae ordered the horses, now, and led us hell-for-leather out on the Perth road on a nicht as black as a sewer and onding of snaw?

ELLIOT: And the claret birling fine and the doxies growing kinder every minute. God's wounds, I never saw a man whose guts led his heid such a dance. What for did you do it?

PHILIP: Oh, that hot room, and the hot claret and the hot wenches! And poor Andrew out there cold and coffined in the frost. I couldna, man, I couldna. I needed the wind in my face. Poor Andrew!

GRANT (*shaking his head in maudlin solemnity*): A good lad was Andy. A good lad.

ELLIOT: Aye, and hotter at this minute than you and I above ground in this blasted, rotting. forfechan midden of a changehouse. Curse my lungs what a drab's kitchen! Where's auld St Patey wi' the aqua-vitae?

PHILIP: He was a bonny singer, was Andy.
(*He weeps.*)

GRANT: He was good company. The best of the whole boiling of us. I wonder, Duncan, you have the heart to flyte.

ELLIOT: By St Paul's breeks, and isna flyting the only thing? There's poor Andra, a fine, swearing, randan, lechering, drinking, guttling young bully-be-damned it did your heart good to see ruffling down the Canongate wi' the beaver of him cockit. None of your pinched Psalmists, yon. Full of blood, the boy was. And Death comes creeping up behind him and grips him by the thrapple in his cups. Andrew, no less. Nae snivelling Whig, like Sneckie here. But a bull of a lad wi' forty years' hard boozing and for-nicketing before him. What can we do but flyte?
(*The* OLD MAN *has come through the door of the tap with*

brandy and glasses. He puts them on the table while Elliot is speaking.)

PHILIP: Lord in heaven, see me some of yon! (*He reels to the table and pours himself a drink. The others drink too, and do honour to his toast. They become quieter and steadier. The effect is most pronounced on Philip, but there is madness in his eyes.*) Death, boys, Death? Here's damnation to Death! ... You don't honour the toast, Mister Innkeeper?

OLD MAN: No. . . . No. Death is a coarse companion, but he sees you home, and aye pays your reckoning.

PHILIP: Damn your companion! D'ye hear? My mother was a bonny lady, and Death bloated her like a drooned dog and took her away raving like a fishwife. My father was a kind man, who prayed each night for Death to take him in a glen with four or five Whigamores at his claymore's point. The false thief, Death, chokit him with a bloody flux in a strange wife's house in Amiens. Lily-white maids and wee croodling weans that never did harm to any, the foul butcher clutches and slays and rots awa their brightness. And he's cut in twa the heart of the best friend I ever had. . . . (*He drinks again.*) You're old. The old ken Death. Day by day they see him face to face. Show me Death, you wizened dog. Show me Death. I've twa-three accounts to settle with him.

(*He draws his hanger.*)

OLD MAN: Keep your hands off me, young sir. I'm over old to be feared.

(PHILIP *has shot his bolt for a while. He staggers and almost falls. The* OLD MAN *leads him to the fireside chair, takes off his cloak, and spreads it over his knees. The other two look at them, pulling heavily at the brandy. The* OLD MAN *goes to the window-seat and sits down. A pause.*)

ELLIOT (*with a hoarse laugh*): Faith, there's a ploy for you! Hunting Death! There's a kittle bit fox now.

PHILIP: Death's a man. There's nothing else in earth or sky could be so bitter bad.

GRANT: That's true. That's a true word you say, Philip Macgillivray. There's them that have seen him, though there's few see him and live. An old grey man, they say . . . like yon.

(*He points with the bottle at the Old Man.*)

ELLIOT: Hey! You'll no be Death, then, Methusalem?

OLD MAN: No. Oh, no.

ELLIOT: Are you acquaint with him, then?

OLD MAN: No, to my sorrow. The long days I've walked the world, restlessly, seeking him! But he will not have my life. Do you ken the verse, you three scholars?

'Thus walk I like a restless caitiff wight,
And on the ground which is my mother's gate
So knock I with my staff, early and late.
And call to her, "Love, Mother, let me in!
Lo, how I vanish, flesh and blood and skin!
Alas! When shall my body be at rest?"'

Gentlemen, you're young. There are happier ways than the gate you have chosen. And for the nicht there is poor cheer for you between these walls. I rede you go home to your beds and pray. And God be with you.

(*He gets up and walks towards the door of the tap.*)

GRANT: Amen. Here endeth the lesson.

(PHILIP *springs up in another gust of passion and gets between the Old Man and the door.*)

PHILIP: No, nor ends! Are you thinking to turn us back, with your sly soft words? Do you think that we are drunk? You wear the white crest of Death on your head. You're in league with him against all youth. Show us our enemy!

ELLIOT (*rising*): Ay, by the Black Plague! There's a fight worth fighting, now. We three against Death, and the deil tak' the chicken-guts! Show us Death, gaffer, or we'll clap your hurdies on your ain bit fire. You'll burn like parchment, cock's body!

OLD MAN: Sit ye down, gentlemen. Wild words are like the wind in the chimney to me. I'm old, ye understand. Sit down. I'll tell ye a thing about Death.

GRANT: Pray silence for Methusalem. Methusalem's going to give us a bawr. A wee bit bawdy in it, Methusalem. Haud your peace, Mr Elliot, for Methusalem's bawr. Sit down, Doctor Macgillivray, if you're no better at standing than that. The court is open.

OLD MAN: Death's in this room. . . . (*A pause.*) I had this house from the heirs of Alec Bain; and Alec Bain was found deid in this room with his heid in the ashes. There. His elder brother, Big John, was pistolled by a highwayman in that chair you sit in. They were taking a dram thegither. Their father, Archibald of the Garse, hanged himself from yon beam. Auld Archie, the great-uncle, who built the place lang syne, died in yon chair too, and it is said the devil took his saul. He hid a peck of siller some place, but it was never found, and it has been an ill job seeking it. It was seeking it that the Bains died. Every man. . . . And now, gentlemen, I cannot refuse you shelter. I have nae beds but my ain, and I'll betake mysel' there now. The logs are under the settle. God be with you, young gentlemen.

(*He goes, taking the lamp with him and closing the door of the tap behind him.*)

PHILIP: If Death should be in this room!

ELLIOT: I'm thinking there's a hantle mair in this room than auld Blood and Banes. Watch the door, Sneckie, and hit the auld carlin on the heid if he comes back. Did ye lippen tae his story?

GRANT (*glass in hand at the taproom door*): Me? I heard nae shtory. Just an ould ballant to nae tune.

ELLIOT (*examining the chimney-piece*): Stash your gab. . . .

So Death came to the Bains at their ain fireside. Now, was not that a droll place for Death to come for the Bains? At their ain fireside. And is't no a droll fireside for the Bains to be at when Death came sleeking in at their back-sides? And is Death no the sly old dog to come aye to the same fireside to drench his garb in blood? Ay, the same fireside. Cock's body, there are more things in heaven and earth . . . And a gey queer bit bastard of a fireside. Master Philip, did they teach ye architecture at the Coallege of Edinburgh? Nay, hogswounds. Naething so useful. Wining and wenching they teach you at the Coallege in Edinburgh. Have ye found Death yet, Philip Adonis Aesculapius, my sweetheart? Ye're a great wee cocksparrow to be ruffling wi' Death. *Mors, pallida mors.* Atch! Come oot, ye besom? And there's the reason what wey Death came for the Bains at their ain fireside! (*He has levered out a large stone with his dagger. He drags a heavy ironbound box from the cavity.*) Ay, by Calvary, a droll place for Death to come for the Bains! (*He crouches on the floor, forcing the lock of the box.*)

PHILIP: Duncan! How did ye ken of this?

ELLIOT: Have I been so long time with you and yet thou hast not known me, Philip? Ratiocination, Philip. Besides, I have a keen nose for the siller. . . . Charlies, by Satan! In bags. There's the bonny, poxy phiz of old Rowley. Yellow wi' the jaundice. Gold, Whig, gold! Cock your snout, Whig! Now comes in the sweet o' the night. (GRANT *joins the group, his eyes starting out of his head.*) Look now. Away you, Philip, and saddle the beasts, if your unruly members will tak you that far. We maun be at the Port of Leith by cock-crow. Haste ye, man. Sneckie and me'll burn the papers and dispose the bags about us. Then we'll settle wi' auld Methusalem. What was his word? 'Death aye pays the lawing.' He'll pay it well this night, mine host! Haste ye, Philip. (PHILIP *goes out to the road, leaving the door half open.*) Look you, Sneckie. Yon lad's owre unchancy ballast for the course we're setting. When he comes back I'll put twa bags in his hands and you'll come on him behind and put a knife between his ribs. Are ye sober enough?

GRANT: Ay, I'm sober.

ELLIOT: Then ye'll do it?

GRANT: Ay, I'll do it.

ELLIOT: Then we'll awa ben and let out the auld runt's life before he wakes. You're sure ye ken what to do?

GRANT: Ay, I ken.

ELLIOT: You heard his talk, the night? He's no companion for a gentleman of fortune. I'd liefer have the hangman. 'Show him Death!' Set him up. He's owre long in the tongue. Come.

(*They go into the taproom.* PHILIP *comes in. He has been hiding behind the door. He is rubbing a handful of snow on his shoulders and face. He is in a foggy, vicious state of drunkenness, but moderately steady in his movements.*)

PHILIP: So. So, my gentlemen. There's friendship! The knife! I heard ye. I heard ye. You'd murder me, you think, you deil's bitches. Wait. Wait. Bide a wee while. They teach you other matters than wining and wenching at Edinburgh College, Mr Duncan Elliot. Where have I it now? Ah, here. Ah, here! Death! Here's Death in a wee box. There you lie, Atropos, the beautiful lady; drown yourself in the brandy. (*He pours the contents of the box into the half-finished glasses of the two murderers.*) Oh, wait you, now, Duncan Elliot, my learned brother. It's the great drinker of spirits you are, certainly, and the fine boastful man of his potations. We'll see how you like the deadly nightshade. The deadly nightshade. . . . Saddle the beasts, says you, Philip Macgillivray, you bloody stable-boy! That'll warm your heart, Duncan, for the long ride to the Port of Leith. Ha, ha, ha! It's a bonny port, the Port of Leith!

(*The* MURDERERS *re-enter.* ELLIOT *wipes his dagger on the tablecloth. Neither can keep his eyes off Philip, and neither can meet his eye.*

ELLIOT: You are very joco.

PHILIP: I'm fine. I'm a man again. Let us drink. Let us drink to Death. Good old Death! Come. Drink. Drink to Death. (*He goes to the table and fills up glasses for Elliot and Grant. He is about to take them up when Elliot grips his wrists and pins them to the table.*

ELLIOT: Now, Sneckie. (GRANT *stabs Philip under the left armpit. Philip makes no sound, but drags himself free from Elliot and falls forward into the fireplace.*) Tchach! What butcher's work. That was well struck, Sneckie. He never gi'ed a grunt. Come. A deoch an doris, and we'll bundle and go.

GRANT: Goad! I need it too. Save us all, what a fine like end to an ambrosial night! (*They stand at opposite sides of the table and drink in great gulps. Suddenly they put down their glasses and look at each other with fear in their eyes.*)

CURTAIN

GLOSSARY

bawr: joke, comic story
beaver: a (top) hat
birling: turning rapidly, carousing
birse: bristle
carlin: old man
croodling: cooing
deoch an doris: (parting) drink
flyte: scold
forfechan: exhausted
fornicketing: fornicating
gaffer: old man
hantle: a great deal
hurdies: buttocks
joco: jocose
kittle: dangerous
liefer: rather

lippen tae: trust, depend on
onding: showering heavily
peck: tidy sum
phiz: face
Old Rowley: nickname for Charles II
randan: carousel
rede: counsel
runt: undersized, thickset person
stoup: flagon, measure of liquor
thrapple: windpipe, throat
wight: mighty
jaud: (old) broken down animal

PRODUCTION NOTES

Something of the simple melodrama of the old Morality plays that feature Death as a character is at the core of this short play. The evil, brutality, and coarseness of human beings are brought out and contrasted with the calm impersonality of the Old Man as Death.

The first brief sequence between Elliot and the Old Man should be vigorously presented to emphasize the atmosphere of cold and Elliot's brutal impatience. The second sequence up to the Old Man's departure has three distinct parts and moods that must be marked. In the first there is contrast between Elliot's noisy exuberance and Grant's discretion; and there is also an isolating of Philip as the one weeping and mourning for their friend Andrew just haled off by Death. In the second part a half-humorous attempt is made to identify the Old Man with Death; and in the third part comes the Old Man's climactic story of the Bains that identifies the room as a place of death. The drama within this narrative will best be brought out by quiet impersonal tones. The final sequence begins on a noisy active note as Elliot punctuates his search for the treasure box by harsh cynical remarks. The speaking here must be carefully synchronized with the rummaging and levering out of the box. Actions are swift after this: Elliot takes charge and orders Philip out to saddle the horses; and the scene narrows to a close intrigue as Elliot and Grant plan the two murders. Here stark lighting concentrating on the two figures will help; and in the same way Philip when he returns and is alone on the stage planning the poisoning will be helped by concentrated lighting. The pinioning and stabbing of Philip will require considerable rehearsing for timing and positioning – especially at the moment of his fall. The remaining dialogue should be completed at a fair pace; and the pause after the drinking must be held long enough to make the audience thrill with the horror of it. A sudden black-out or a gradual dimming-out could be equally effective.

TALKING POINTS

On Staging and Acting

1. What directions would you give each of the three men –
   Elliot, Grant, MacGillivray – to help to mark the differ-
   ences in character and personality in the very first scene?
   Consider such things as tone of voice, gestures, movements, relative positions.
2. Consider how movements, gestures, and grouping would
   help to create atmosphere for the old man's recital of the
   story of the Bains.
3. How would you overcome the practical problem of siting
   and unearthing the 'heavy ironbound box'? How would
   you have Elliot positioned at this point, and what directions would you give him?
4. Work out in detail Philip MacGillivray's actions and
   movements as he prepares the poison. Remember that
   all the significant actions must be seen clearly by the
   audience.
5. By diagram and explanatory notes show how the murder
   of MacGillivray might be staged.
6. Consider the grouping and the build-up of atmosphere in
   the final scene. What touches would you add to point the
   melodrama of the conclusion?

On the Human Situation

1. A Morality was supposed to teach a lesson about vice and
   virtue. How far is this play a successful Morality?
2. Honour among thieves.

3. Consider the use of the word 'death' and the figure of the Old Innkeeper.
4. Try to place the three ruffians in order of evil, the worst first.
5. How apt and inventive is the dialogue, and especially for evoking the period and differentiating the characters?

Hewers of Coal

A Drama in One Act

by

JOE CORRIE

Joe Corrie (1894–1968), a Fife miner, was a powerful influence in the Scottish Community Drama movement and its annual competitive festivals. His first plays were written during the General Strike of 1926 for the Bowhill Village Players. With his actor miners he toured the music halls of Scotland and the north of England from 1929–31. Although he wrote full length plays, poems and a novel, his finest gifts were revealed in his one-act plays. Of those with a contemporary setting, *Hewers of Coal* written in 1931 is the best. Self-taught, with a natural flair for exploiting conflict, both serious and comic, he can give significance to the seemingly ordinary words and actions of seemingly ordinary men and women.

PERSONS IN THE PLAY

In order of appearance

DICK, *a miner of middle age*
BILLIE, *a boy of fifteen years*
PETER, *a pit handyman, fifty years of age*
JOE, *a miner of middle age*
BOB, *a gaffer, fifty years of age*

SCENE ONE: *A 'Heading' Underground*
SCENE TWO: *The Old Hard Coal Heading*
TIME: *Twentieth Century*

Applications regarding performance of this play should be addressed to J. Garnet Miller Ltd and Steel's Play Bureau, 1–5 Portpool Lane, London E.C.1. No performance may be given unless permission has first been obtained.

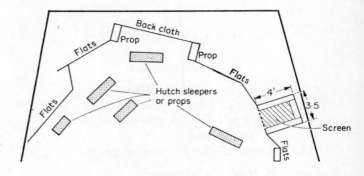

Flats represent walls of mine; backcloth suggests coal face. Heavy cloth overhead representing low ceiling slopes downwards towards back of stage to height of 5 ft 6 in. The second scene is an even more confined chamber which can be suggested by moving forwards the flats on the right (spectator's left), lowering the overhead cloth, and dropping a second (black) backcloth. To suggest irregularity of floor, a sloping platform may be pushed on for this second scene.

HEWERS OF COAL

NOTE. As different districts have different underground names and expressions, the producer may have to alter the words to suit his particular audience.

SCENE: *A 'heading' underground. It is a narrowly confined place about five feet six inches high, hewn out of the solid rock. A narrow strip of coal can be seen along the whole length of the back wall. A couple of props are at the back, a jacket hanging to a nail in one.*

The only entrance is in the right (spectator's) wall. This is an opening about four feet high, and three and a half feet wide, with a prop at each side of it and one across the top. Over this opening there hangs a coarse and dirty canvas 'screen' – one of the underground precautions for a better air current. A few old hutch sleepers and pieces of prop lie here and there, on which the men sit when they are taking their meal.

When the curtain rises DICK *sits in the centre eating bread and cheese from a 'piece-tin', and drinking from a tea-flask. At his side there is a larger can which holds water. At right (spectator's)* BILLIE *sits, also at his meal. They have been in the pit for three hours and their faces are black. Both have donned their coats, as is the custom in the mine when men are having their meal. Their safety lamps are beside them, but there should be a dim blue light added for stage purposes.*

BILLIE, *with his mouth full, puts his 'piece-tin' together and closes it with a snap. He puts it in his pocket as much as to say, 'Well, that's that.'* DICK *still taking his meal, looks round at Billie.*

DICK: Finished with your meal already, Billie?

BILLIE (*still chewing*): M-m!

DICK: You shouldn't eat so quick, lad, it isn't good for the stomach.

BILLIE: I've got a stomach that can digest nails. . . . Peter's taking a long time to come in for his ham and egg.

DICK: There's a smash-up of hutches down the slope. Didn't you know that?

BILLIE: That's why the haulage was stopped before stopping time?

DICK: Yes. Some smash, too, Peter'll be cursing, for he doesn't care about losing sweat, the lazy . . .

(*The fact that Billie is a boy keeps him from expressing himself to the full.*)

BILLIE (*who has been eyeing Dick's tin*): Is that scone you have with you?

DICK: Yes. (*Smiling.*) Want a bit?

(BILLIE *needs no second bidding. He is at Dick's side immediately.* DICK, *still smiling, hands him a piece of the scone.* BILLIE *takes a large bite.*)

BILLIE: Thanks, Dick – a million!

(*He returns to his former seat enjoying the scone to the full.*)

DICK: You seem to be fond of scone, Billie?

BILLIE: I could eat it till it was coming out o' my ears. . . . It was a bad day for me when my mother died, Dick. (*Sighs.*) She used to bake scones every day.

DICK: Doesn't your sister do any baking?

BILLIE (*full of scorn*): Her! She hasn't time to bake for powdering her face and waving her hair. Pictures and dancing, that's all *she* can think about. Mad to get a man, Dick, and when she does get one she'll poison him with tinned meat. I've got a new name for her now.

DICK (*amused*): Oh, what have you christened her, Billie?

BILLIE (*with great satisfaction*): Tin-opener Trixie. By gum!

she's an expert at it. The back of our house is like a munition work with empty tins.

DICK (*still amused*): They tell me she's a champion dancer?

BILLIE: Dancer, yes, but it isn't round a baking-board. (*Pause.*) This scone is just great, Dick. You must be proud of your wife?

DICK (*suddenly thoughtful*): Not as proud as I should be, perhaps. . . . The miner is a thoughtless kind o' fellow, Bill. He goes home on pay day with about forty shillings, hands it over to the missus like a hero, forgetting that the Chancellor o' the Exchequer himself would have to throw in the sponge if he had to feed and clothe a man, a wife, and five kiddies on it. How the hell they manage to keep their head above water is a mystery to me. . . . And yet they have the heart to laugh and sing, too.

BILLIE: My mother was always singing, Dick – always. (*With downcast eyes.*) By gum! I *do* miss her.

DICK: Is your father keeping better now?

BILLIE (*rather hopelessly*): Some days he's all right, other days he's all wrong. I don't think he'll ever get right now.

DICK: You've had a rotten time, Billie, between one thing and another.

BILLIE: Father says that we're lucky with me working. It helps to keep us going. So I'll have to try and keep my job, Dick.

DICK (*thoughtfully*): A job! . . . The whole world seems to go round on a job. . . . No job, no bread – no bread, no laughter. (*Sighs.*) It's a strange way of running a world, in my opinion.

(*There is a slight pause. Then we hear a pony neighing outside.* BILLIE *looks at Dick quite tragically.*)

BILLIE: That's Danny. . . . And I forgot to keep him a piece o' my bread.

DICK (*lightly*): He has plenty of oats, Bill.

BILLIE: He looks forward now to getting a bit o' my bread and a drink o' my tea. (*Pony neighs again.*) He and I are great pals, Dick. If ever I win a big coupon I'm going to buy him from the company and take him up to the green fields. (*Pleadingly, in a way.*) It was greedy of me eating all my bread and not thinking o' Danny, wasn't it?

(DICK *holds out the last piece of scone he has left.*)

DICK: Take that out to him, Billie.

(BILLIE *immediately rises to get it.*)

BILLIE (*taking it*): Dick, you're Public Hero Number One.

(*He goes towards the exit.*)

DICK: Lift that screen, Billie, and give us a breath of air. It's beginning to suffocate in here.

(*While* BILLIE *is lifting the screen to hang it up the pony neighs again.*)

BILLIE: I'm coming, Danny – I'm coming!

(BILLIE *goes off.* DICK *wipes his brow with his fingers and throws the sweat off them. Then he takes a long breath or two of the air which seems to be coming in now. He closes his tin, and puts it and his tea-flask in his jacket pockets.* PETER *enters. He is in his shirt sleeves, rolled up and is wiping his brow with a red and white spotted handkerchief.* DICK *is conscious of his entrance but doesn't look at him.* PETER *speaks on entering and goes to his jacket, which is hanging on the prop. He rolls down his sleeves and speaks in Dick's direction.*)

PETER: The things that happen down this pit would break the heart of a saint.

(*He takes his flask and tin from his pockets.*)

DICK (*looking up at him unpleasantly*): What's the matter with you?

PETER: Didn't you see that smash at the bottom o' the slope? Four hutches broke away from that last race and jammed themselves right up to the roof. . . . Where's that boy?

DICK: What d' ye want with him?

PETER: The gaffer's coming up to speak to him about it. He put a coupling on twisted – that caused the break-away. I wouldn't be surprised if he gets the sack – Robert's flaming about it.

DICK: And how did Robert know it was a twisted coupling that caused the smash?

PETER: I told him.

DICK (*getting angry*): And how did you know?

PETER: Because it was the only way it *could* come off.

(PETER *sits at left to have his meal.*)

DICK (*angry*): You're damned ready at spotting things like that for the gaffer, aren't ye? D'you think he loves you for it?

PETER: Who are *you* barking at?

DICK: You! The lad wouldn't put a coupling on twisted intentionally, would he? Mistakes *will* happen. Have you never made one in your life?

PETER: If you saw the mess that I had to clear up you wouldn't be so damned kind.

DICK: Isn't it your job in this pit to clear up messes? And, if you want my opinion, you're well suited to the job. Get what I mean?

PETER: Look here, Dick! If there's going to be any more o' this talks at meals I'm going to talk to the gaffer about it. I'm not going to stand insults from you.

DICK: If Billie gets the sack because o' this you'll have to stand a damned sight more than insults – I'll break your blasted neck.

PETER: It's no business o' yours, anyhow.

DICK: I'm *making* it my business. That lad can't afford to lose his job – it's the only thing between his family and starvation. Why did you tell the gaffer he was to blame?

PETER: If I had kept the blame off him it might have fallen on me.

DICK: Yes, and that would have been a hell of a tragedy, wouldn't it? You with your extra shifts and your ham and egg – you selfish swine!

PETER: If a man doesn't look after himself in this pit nobody else will.

DICK (*scornfully*): Is that your outlook on life?

PETER: It is.

DICK: There might come a day, Peter, when *you*'ll be depending on the help of someone. What'll you do then?

PETER: That day will *never* come – don't worry about that.

DICK: Better men than you have needed help, and have been damned glad to accept it when it *did* come.

PETER: Well, there's one thing you can be sure of, Dick. It'll be a bad day for me when I'm looking for help from *you*.

DICK: Don't boast, Peter. This is a strange world, remember, and some strange things happen in it.

PETER: That's *one* thing that'll never happen.

(BILLIE *returns. He immediately sniffs and looks at Peter, who is now busy eating.*)

BILLIE: There's a grand smell o' ham and egg in here.

DICK: Ten shifts a week and no kiddies to keep. Makes a difference, Billie.

(PETER *glances unkindly at Dick for a moment, then looks at Billie.*)

PETER (*to Billie*): Did you see the gaffer out there?

BILLIE (*puzzled*): No. . . . What does he want with me?

DICK: You're getting the blame o' that smash.

BILLIE: Me? How?

PETER: You put a coupling on twisted and it came off going over the brow.

(BILLIE *is troubled.*)

BILLIE (*to Dick*): Does that mean I'll get the sack?

DICK: If you have to go up the pit today, Bill, you won't be the only one.

BILLIE: What d'you mean, Dick?

DICK: Never mind just now. . . . Doesn't Joe know it's stopping-time?

BILLIE: He's not taking his food in here today.

DICK: Why not?

BILLIE: I don't know. He took his food into the coal face this morning.

DICK: Go and give him a shout, anyhow, and make sure that he's all right.

(BILLIE *goes off, giving Peter a nasty look as he goes.*)

DICK: Billie's father's ill – you know that?

PETER: Well?

DICK: They're just scraping through on Billie's wage.

PETER: What has that to do with me?

DICK: You can tell the gaffer that you found a broken link on the slope, and that *it* caused the smash?

PETER: Yes, and if it was found out that I was telling the gaffer a lie it would mean the sack for *me*.

DICK: If Billie gets the sack because of this I'll—

(BOB *enters. He is a tall man wearing short leggings. He hangs his lamp on his belt.*)

BOB (*to Peter*): There's a loose strand in that haulage rope. Get your splicing tools and run it in before starting-time.

(PETER *immediately closes his tin, rises, and hurries off.*)

PETER: I'll not be a minute, Robert . . . no more than a minute.

(PETER *goes off.* BOB *takes a note-book and pencil from his pocket and writes something down.*)

BOB: If it isn't one thing down here it's two. That's half an hour lost this morning.

DICK: Of course, a coal pit isn't like a biscuit works, Bob, where everything goes like a song?

BOB: There's too much carelessness. And I'm going to make an example this morning. Where's that pony driver?

DICK: He's in telling Joe Marshall to come in here for his meal.

BOB: Well, you can tell him not to start work until I speak to him.

DICK: Thinking of sacking him, are ye?

BOB: That smash was his fault and he'll have to pay for it.

DICK: Mistakes can happen with all of us, Bob.

BOB: We can't afford them happening with us.

DICK (*amused*): We! Us! When did you get a share in the Imperial Coal Company, Bob?

(BOB *looks at Dick quickly.*)

BOB: What d' you mean?

DICK: You said 'we' – 'us.' Only the directors speak in the plural.

BOB: Oh, being sarcastic, eh? Cut it out, Dick, or you might be getting more fresh air than is good for the health.

DICK: So you *do* know what fresh air is?

BOB: Eh?

DICK: We could be doing with a lot more of it down here.

BOB (*after looking at the entrance with the screen up*): Seems to me you're getting a damned sight more than your share.

(*He goes to the entrance and lets the screen drop angrily.*)

DICK (*with a smile*): It would be fine if everything in this pit could be remedied as easily as that, Bob – eh?

BOB: What are ye driving at?

DICK: Have you got that fall cleared up in the main aircourse yet?

BOB: What the hell have you to do with the main aircourse?

DICK: I was just trying to get information.

BOB: Well, what'll happen to me if it isn't cleared up?

DICK: It isn't what'll happen to you – it's what'll happen to the lot of us. (*Significantly.*) There's no shortage o' gas down here, remember.

BOB (*with a sarcastic smile*): Is that so?

DICK: There's a shortage o' props, a shortage o' air, but no shortage o' gas.

BOB (*thoughtfully*): I see! . . . Dick, come into my office at finishing-time. I want a serious talk with you.

(PETER *returns carrying his splicing tools in his hand.*)

PETER: I'm ready, Robert.

(BOB *goes to the exit, stops and looks back at Dick.*)

BOB: Gas in the pit, is there? And a fall in the main aircourse. And you'd like the Government inspector to know about it – eh? I have a way of dealing with your kind, Dick. Keep mind o' that.

(BOB *goes off.* PETER *follows like a dog at the heels of its master.* DICK *smiles, but it is a troubled smile.* BILLIE *enters.*)

BILLIE: Am I to get the sack, Dick?

DICK: Leave that to me, Bill. . . . Is Joe coming in?

BILLIE: Yes. But he's had his meal, Dick; he took it at the coal-face.

DICK: He has never done that before.

BILLIE: He said he was too hungry to wait till stopping-time. (BILLIE *sits.*) If I get the sack I'll be afraid to go home, Dick.

DICK: If you get the sack today, Billie, I'll bring this bloody pit out on strike. And the company would have something to say about *that*.

(JOE *enters. He doesn't look at all well, and has a racking cough.*)

DICK: That cough o' yours is getting worse, Joe.

JOE (*struggling for breath*): That air down there is killing me, Dick – killing me.

DICK: Why do you work in it?

JOE: I wouldn't if I could get out of it. . . . But he knows he has me there, and won't give me another job. . . . I wish to God I had never married, Dick – it has been hell ever since . . . being chained down here.

DICK: They know when they have a lever all right. (JOE *sits where Peter was sitting*.) Why didn't you take your breakfast with us?

JOE (*guiltily*): I . . . took it early.

DICK: Why?

JOE: My place was on the move . . . and I had to come out to see if it would settle. . . . And I can't get any wood to secure it. (*Hysterically*.) Dick! . . . I'm getting afraid to work in there. . . . It'll come down some day and crush me to pulp!

(DICK *is alarmed at this outburst*. BILLIE *just looks at Joe in a puzzled way*. DICK *goes to Joe*.)

DICK: Joe, you've got to pull yourself together, lad – you're letting your nerves get the better of ye.

JOE: But I can't help it! . . . I know it'll come down on me and . . .

DICK: I know what's the matter this morning, Joe. It's hunger. You didn't *bring* a meal with you this morning?

JOE: No, Dick, I . . . I . . .

DICK: It's all right, Joe, you needn't be ashamed of it. It's no crime to come to the pit without bread when there's a wife and kiddies to come first. (DICK *looks at Billie*.) (*To Billie*.) Peter left a bit of his bread for the pony, didn't he?

BILLIE (*astounded*): What, *he* did?

DICK (*nodding his head to Billie on the quiet*): You were out at the time and didn't hear him. . . . Danny has plenty of oats. (DICK *lifts Peter's bread tin, takes the bread from it, and pushes it into Joe's hand*. JOE *shrinks from it*.)

JOE: No! . . . Peter would tell it all through the pit!

DICK (*forcing it into his hand*): Take it and don't be a bloody fool! . . . I'll explain to Peter, and it'll be all right. (JOE *takes it, but reluctantly and ashamed*.) If you don't want to take it here go into the coal-face and eat it.

(JOE *looks at Dick in a hopeless manner*.)

JOE: Dick, I'm tired. . . . I'm not fit enough now to be working here, but – there's nothing else for it. . . . If that roof *would* come down and put an end to me Mary would get compensation, and her troubles would be all over.

DICK: Joe! Get that idea out of your head. That's the coward's way out. . . . Go and eat that bread – it'll do you a world of good. (JOE *rises and goes off slowly. We hear him coughing when he has gone.*) Joe's just about a goner, I think.

BILLIE: Peter 'll be mad when he finds his bread missing.

DICK (*with a smile*): We'll blame it on the rats, Billie. He has enough ham and egg in him anyway to last him for the rest o' the shift. If he hasn't it'll do him good to feel hungry for once.

(PETER *returns hurrying and still cross.*)

PETER (*entering*): It's little wonder my meals never do *me* any good. I never get peace to sit down to them. Always something going wrong. (*He sits in his previous position. He lifts his tin, getting a shock at the lightness of it. He looks suspiciously at Dick. Then he opens the tin.*) Here! What has happened to my bread?

DICK: A couple of rats came in and took it away, Peter.

PETER (*sarcastically*): Oh, did they? Opened the lid, then shut it after them, eh?

DICK: Yes. They're getting more human down here every day.

(PETER *rises threateningly.*)

PETER: Where's my bread?

DICK (*to Billie*): Doesn't believe a word I say nowadays, Billie.

PETER: I want that bread back – see!

DICK: Too late, Peter, it's away ta-ta.

PETER: Where is it?

DICK: Well, Joe Marshall came in here and I discovered that he didn't bring a slice with him to the pit. So I thought you wouldn't mind him having what you had left.

PETER: What! You gave my bread away to him! . . . And what am I going to do now?

DICK: I think you had a good tightener.

(PETER *lifts his tin madly and raises it above Dick.*)

PETER: I'll bring this down on your blasted head, you . . .

(DICK *protects himself.* BILLIE *jumps.* ROBERT *enters.*)

BOB: What's the matter here?

(PETER *looks at Bob piteously.*)

PETER (*whining*): Robert, he stole the bread from my tin when I was out and gave it away.

BOB (*puzzled*): Stole your bread?

PETER: Stole it and gave it to Joe Marshall.

BOB (*to Dick*): Is this true?

DICK: Joe came in here dead beat with hunger. I thought that Peter would be only too pleased to do a good turn to a mate for once in his life.

PETER (*still whining*): He didn't even ask my permission, Robert. . . . And here I am, left without a slice.

BOB: Dick, pack up your tools and get up the pit. (*To Billie.*) And you do the same.

DICK: Right-o! But before I *do* go I'm going to knock the head off this greedy swine.

(DICK *angrily divests himself of his jacket,* BOB *gets between him and Peter.* PETER *slinks back to a corner.*)

BOB (*to Dick*): You know what it means to strike a man down a pit?

DICK (*making towards Peter, and trying to get past Bob*): I don't care! Joe was hungry and . . .

(*There is heard a terrific roar, like thunder. Immediately the quarrel is forgotten. Like trapped animals they instinctively herd together and rush to the left wall.* BILLIE *rushes to the shelter of Dick. The noise gets louder and more terrible. There is a pause, then* JOE *staggers in, falls, then crawls towards his mates.*)

JOE: We're trapped – trapped!

(*The noise is now horrible, and the falling of debris is heard. A stone, accompanied by a cloud of dust, falls on the scene. A loud crash is heard at the entrance.*)

(*Gradually the noise begins to fade, like thunder among the hills. Then quietness falls, save for the echo of falling debris in the working around.*)

(DICK *goes cautiously to the entrance. He lifts the screen. They all give a start, for the way out is blocked by fallen stone.* DICK *turns and looks at his stricken mates.*)

DICK: God! ... We're entombed!

A SLOW CURTAIN

SCENE TWO

Immediately after the close of the curtain, through the darkness, we hear the voice of a wireless announcer.

ANNOUNCER: This is the National Programme. ... The death roll in the Glendinning pit disaster has now reached forty-two, two other bodies have been found this morning. For the past five days the rescue parties have worked in relays, day and night. They are endeavouring now to reach the Hard Coal Heading, which, it is thought, a few of the men may have reached through old workings. Little hope, however, is being held of finding the men alive. Messages of sympathy have been received from his Majesty the King, the Prime Minister, the Minister for Mines, and the Archbishop of Cravenbury. A relief fund has been opened for the bereaved relatives to relieve the destitution, and contributions will be gratefully received at the office of the Miners' Federation, or may be sent to the Provost of Glendinning. ... In the South Wales coalfield another strike has broken out, the men claiming an increase of wages. The strike is entirely unofficial and . . .

(*The last few words fade out as the curtain gradually opens.*)

The scene is the old Hard Coal Heading. It is on a slope, rising from right to left. This can be done by using a sloped platform, a sloped frontpiece from about one foot at right to over two feet at left, with an irregular top edging to resemble coal. A black curtain can be lowered from the top at a corresponding angle.

There is a small opening at right, but it is only a hole big enough for a man to crawl through. It is no outlet to the world, as the workings around are all closed. The first thing to strike the eye will be five chalked strokes on the back wall.

There is only one lamp alight, hanging near DICK, *who sits in the centre rather like a Rodin sculpture.* BOB *is at right on his knees, putting up a silent prayer.* BILLIE *lies asleep between Bob and Dick.* JOE *lies to left of Dick, also asleep, and looking deathly pale.* PETER *is at extreme left, looking hopelessly at the wall at left. They all wear their jackets, and it is easily seen that they are nearly done. It is the courage of Dick that has saved them up till now, that and the water-can which is close to Dick.*

BOB (*just a faint whisper*): Amen!

(*There is a dead pause for a moment or two.* BOB *looks at Dick pleadingly.*)

BOB: Can I have a few drops o' water, Dick?

(DICK *slowly lifts the can to his ear and shakes it.*)

DICK: It can only *be* a drop or two, Bob.

BOB: I know.

DICK: Today'll finish it.

(DICK *hands the can over to Bob.* PETER *looks on the scene with staring eyes. While* BOB *sips,* PETER *begins to crawl towards him.* DICK *watches him closely.* BOB *hands the can back to Dick.*)

PETER: Can I wet my tongue, too, Dick? (DICK *looks at Joe.*)

DICK: I'm afraid we'll have to keep the rest for Joe. . . .

You've had your share today, Peter. . . . I'm worried about Joe, he looks done for.

PETER (*piteously*): Oh! . . . Just two drops, Dick – for God's sake!

(DICK *is sorry for him.*)

DICK: All right, but it must be your last – absolutely.

PETER: I know.

(DICK *gives Peter the water-can, but holds on to it. He pulls it away when he thinks Peter has taken enough.* PETER *returns to his former position. There is a pause. Then* BOB *crawls to Dick and takes hold of his hand.*)

BOB: Dick – before it is too late. . . . Thanks for all you have done for us. . . . It was your pluck that got us here . . . your hope that has kept us alive . . . if it has failed . . . Oh!

DICK: It might have been better if we had stayed where we were – it would have been all over now. . . . But life is sweet. . . . Still, we know each other better now – and that's something.

BOB: Yes, but it's a pity we don't know more of the good things in life until it's too late.

(BOB *returns to his former position. There is a pause.*)

BOB (*hopelessly*): Not a sound – anywhere!

DICK (*quickly*): Listen! (DICK, PETER, *and* BOB *are all attention to listen. After a pause, hopelessly.*) No!

BOB: No!

PETER: No!

BOB: Strange that the hunger has passed away.

DICK (*with a faint smile*): It was hellish while it lasted. . . . No craving for food now – just water.

PETER (*a sudden outburst, wildly*): I'm burning inside like a fire – roasting! (*He makes a sudden attempt to get the water-can.* DICK *gets hold of it.* BOB *is prepared to defend Dick. Madly.*) Give me that water! . . . Give me that water – or I'll kill ye! (BOB *lifts a stone from the floor and raises it above his head.*)

BOB: Touch that water, and it'll be your last.

DICK (*who is really master of the situation*): Bob! No temper.
(PETER *goes back to his place.*)

PETER: Oh, this is unbearable – unbearable! (*Then in desperation he beats his hands against the wall.*) Help! Help! Help!

DICK: Cut that out! D'ye want to waken the kid?
(PETER *sinks exhausted.* BOB *and* DICK *both look at the sleeping boy.*)

BOB: Hasn't he been plucky, Dick?

DICK: Plucky? By God, he has!

PETER (*very slowly*): Oh! this waiting – waiting on something that can never happen now . . . waiting!

DICK: Listen! (*Again they are all attention. There is a slight pause.*) No!

BOB (*very tired*): Imagination again. . . . I wonder what has been happening? . . . How many have lost their lives? . . . And they'll be blaming me! (*Hysterically.*) They'll be blaming me!

PETER (*also hysterical*): And you *were* to blame! . . . The main aircourse was never kept clear.

DICK: We were all to blame for something. If it wasn't greed and selfishness, it was fear and cowardice. . . . Thinking only of ourselves, and the others could go to hell. (*To Bob.*) And what has it been worth today?

BOB: If I live to come through this I'll be a different man, Dick.

DICK: We'll all be different men, I think.
(*There is a silence. Then* JOE *begins to rave in his delirium.*)

JOE: Three hundred quid! . . . She'll get three hundred quid! . . . Mary, tell the kiddies that you'll get three hundred quid.
(JOE *laughs very weakly. The others look at him in suspense and fear.*)

BOB (*in a whisper*): He's started again.

DICK (*to Bob*): Is he too weak now to go mad?

PETER (*hysterically*): Mad! ... Oh, my God, we'd have to kill him!

DICK: Peter, haven't you got one single kind thought in that miserable heart o' yours? In a short time we'll all be knocking at the door of Kingdom Come. Let's go with clean hands and hearts.

(PETER *is ashamed.*)

JOE: Three hundred quid of compensation – the price of a dead miner! Three hundred quid, Mary, and – a corpse. ... Ha, ha!

PETER: I can't stand this, I tell ye! – I can't!

(*Again he beats his hands against the stone wall of his prison. Then he gives it up in absolute despair. There is another silence.* BILLIE *begins to talk in his sleep.* DICK *and* JOE *look at him.*)

BILLIE: Mother! ... Mother! ... Dick says that I've been brave. ... You always told me to play the man. ... Dick says I've been great. ... Danny was killed ... my pony ... We were great pals, mother.

DICK: Plucky kid! (*Softly.*) Sleep, Billie ... sleep.

(*A silence.*)

JOE: And Peter grudged me his bit o' bread. ... (*Peter rises as if his conscience had stricken him.*) And I was hungry. ... Oh, I was hungry. ...

PETER (*piteously*): I didn't grudge him my bread, Dick, did I?

DICK: No, Peter, it was all a mistake. You were angry because I didn't ask your permission. Forget about it.

JOE: Three hundred quid! ...

(JOE *tries to sing a word or two of* Love's Old Sweet Song, *but he only gets a few notes out when he stops exhausted. There is a pause.*)

BOB (*quietly*): The sun! ... Just to look up again at the sky! To walk through the woods! ... To climb the hills! ... To lie down and drink the clear, cold water! (*The mention of water makes* PETER *rise again and cast an envious eye on the water-can.* DICK *holds it tightly to himself.*) Five days in hell! And every day an eternity.

DICK: Give me your book and pencil, Bob. I'm going to write to Elsie again. (BOB *gives him the book and pencil.* DICK *begins to write, after counting the chalk marks on the wall. Slowly as he writes.*) Friday – the fifth day. . . . Water now finished – keeping a drop for Joe . . . Billie sleeps – Joe very weak. . . . Last lamp now burning. . . . Still – hoping. . . . Don't worry. . . . Good night, Elsie. . . . Kiss the kids for me. (*Overcome.*) Oh! merciful Christ!

(*This outburst brings both* BOB *and* PETER *to attention, for it is the first.*)

BOB (*quickly*): Dick, for God's sake don't let yourself go like that! Don't let us down now.

(DICK *raises his head, and smiles.*)

DICK: I'm sorry. . . . It was the thought of the kiddies.

(*He tears the leaf from the book, and puts it in his breast-pocket. He gives Bob the book and pencil.* BOB *begins writing his letter.*) (JOE *opens his eyes and stares blankly round the cavern. Gradually he realizes where he is.*)

JOE: Dick . . . can I have a drop o' water – water?

DICK: Sure, Joe. (DICK *goes to him with the can.*) Have you had a good sleep?

JOE: Yes . . . I don't know. . . .

(*He tries to put his hand to his head but is too weak.* DICK *holds the water-can to Joe's lips.* PETER *keeps looking at Joe in an attitude of fear.* DICK *lets Joe have all the water save for a drop or two which he is keeping for Billie. He returns to his seat with the can.* JOE *looks at Peter.*)

JOE: Peter – I didn't eat your bread. (*They are all surprised at this.*) I didn't eat it . . . I put it in my box for the kids . . . and it was buried . . . buried in the fall. (DICK *and* BOB *exchange glances.* JOE *tries to laugh, but only coughs.*) Dick, I'm done for.

DICK: No fear, Joe. You'll live to sing a song yet on the Saturday night – eh?

JOE: Saturday – pay-day – bread – and margarine. Ha, ha!

PETER: I didn't grudge you my bread, Joe, I . . . didn't.

JOE: I'm cold . . . cold.

(PETER *to the surprise of* DICK *and* BOB, *feels Joe's hand.*)

PETER (*softly*): Cold!

(*He takes off his jacket and puts it over Joe.* DICK *nods his head to Bob in a well-pleased manner. There is a short pause, then* PETER *returns to his corner.* DICK *looks at the lamp.*)

DICK: That lamp can't burn much longer. . . . We should put it out and save it.

BOB: No! I couldn't face the dark!

PETER: You might not get it to light again!

DICK: Well, when it does go out, we'll know that the end *has* come.

(BILLIE *raises his head, opening, and rubbing his eyes. He looks all round him, then sinks down again with a little cry of hopelessness.*)

DICK (*comforting Billie*): You told your mother that you had been a man, Billie. . . . That's the spirit my lad. You're made of the right stuff. I kept the last of the water for you, Billie. Have it now?

BILLIE: Yes. (*He sits up and* DICK *lets him drain the can. The others hopelessly watch it go down.*) Anybody been here, Dick?

DICK: Not yet, Bill, but they'll be here soon now.

BOB (*to Billie*): How d' you feel, Billie?

BILLIE: Okay!

BOB: You're a great little fellow.

BILLIE: You won't give me the sack now, Bob?

(*He smiles, having now no fear of the gaffer.*)

BOB: I'll never give any one the sack now, Billie – I'm through with gaffering. (BILLIE *looks up at the lamp suddenly. All look.*)

BILLIE: That lamp's going down!

(*It is flickering slightly. All stare at it tragically. There is a profound silence.*)

JOE (*very quietly*): Three hundred quid. And I thought I was only worth a few shillings. Ha!

BILLIE (*looking at Joe half in fear*): What's wrong with Joe, Dick?

DICK: Just dreaming, Billie.

BILLIE: But his eyes are open – look!

DICK (*to take Billie's attention off Joe*): Shall we have another little sing-song – eh! . . . What'll we sing this time? . . . Our favourite again. . . . One – two; (*Sings.*)

'Speed, bonnie boat, like a bird on the wing,
    Onward, the sailors cry,
Carry the lad that's born to be king,
    Over the sea to Skye.'

(BILLIE *joins* JOE, *then* BOB, *then* PETER. *It is a terrible struggle for them to sing, and the tune is just recognizable but* **no** *more. They are all affected by it, as they feel that it is the last song that will ever come from their lips.*

They are near the end of the verse when DICK *stops suddenly and listens. The others do the same.*)

DICK: Listen (DICK *lifts a piece of stone from the floor and taps with it steadily for a few moments on the rock bottom.*) Listen! (*They put their ears to the floor. Through the stillness we can hear a very faint tapping away somewhere in the distance.* DICK *rises first.*) It's the rescue party – we're saved! We're saved! (*They just look at each other in dumb amazement.*)

BILLIE: Mother! Mother!

DICK: Sing like hell! . . . They *must* hear us! . . . Sing! . . . Sing! (*A superhuman strength possesses them now. They sing quite loudly, looking left.* DICK *stops and holds his hands for silence.*

They listen breathlessly. Far away we can hear the rescue party singing the same song.) They've heard us! Shout! . . . Hooray! . . . Hooray! (*They all shout with the exception of* JOE *who is still motionless.*) Elsie! . . . Elsie! . . . We're saved. . . . (*Overcome with the excitement he shakes* JOE *to awaken him.*) Joe! . . . Joe! . . . They're here at last. . . . They're quite near! . . . They've heard us! . . . We're . . . (*He stops suddenly.*) My God!

(BOB, DICK, *and* PETER *exchange glances.* BILLIE *is puzzled.*

DICK (*to keep the truth from Billie*): We'll just let him sleep, Bob.

BOB: All right.

(*There is a pause, then* DICK *removes his cap.* BOB *follows suit, then* PETER. BILLIE *watches them and does likewise. The lamp flickers more now and will soon be out. In the distance we can hear the tapping of the rescuers, still singing the song.*

THE CURTAIN FALLS SLOWLY

PRODUCTION NOTES

Simplicity and naturalness are the keynotes of this mining play that encloses a tragedy within its drama of rescue. The setting with its low sloping ceiling and projecting walls should give a feeling of oppressiveness, of life in a confined space. It would help if the players learned to walk and move in a stooping, crouching manner.

Particular attention would have to be paid to the character study of Dick. He dominates the play in a quiet insistent way by the power of his personality and leadership. In a way the pace of the production will illustrate the different facets of Dick's personality – gentle in the first sequence with the boy Billy, faster as his anger is aroused in the dialogue with Peter, controlled in his argument with Bob the gaffer, more intense in his sympathetic handling of Joe. Production should bring out three big moments of tension before the quarrel at the end of the first scene – Dick's outburst against Peter, Bob's quiet threat in reply to Dick's challenge ('come into my office . . .') and Joe's hysterical outburst of fear. Near the end of the scene pace should be whipped up to the point where Dick and Peter get ready to fight each other; and the effects men should be carefully drilled to come in with those crashing noises in the middle, not at the end, of Dick's speech: 'Joe was angry . . .' It would be even more effective if the setting were seen to move and shudder, and if the lighting were dipped, to synchronize with the blasts.

The brief interlude – the excerpt from a news bulletin reporting the pit disaster – is best presented in a darkened theatre on a tape recorder. The recorded voice official and metallic will then be contrasted with the real live voices of the people on the stage. As faint lighting picks out the second scene – 'old Hard Coal Heading' – five chalked strokes on the back wall – denoting five days – must become gradually visible in an even more cramped setting. The men's voices must sound weak, but out of their subdued dialogue bursts of hysteria or dream-talk must come suddenly and sharply to stress the atmosphere of tension and suffering. Dick is in control of the situation, and should be played quietly and confidently, so that his momentary break-down is all the more startling to the others. Lighting should be sufficiently subdued and controlled as to suggest the flickering of the lamp; and the attempt to take minds off Joe's plight and cheer up the group by singing should have some spirit in it to begin with but should begin to flag just as the first faint tapping is heard. Pauses are most important here: 'Listen'; and then the renewed burst of singing must have considerable power. Perhaps again a tape recorder could be used here – for the echoing chorus by the rescue party. Dick's final speech will require special rehearsal: he has to strike a loud excited note; and then as he looks at Joe, he gradually breaks off, quietens down, and groans out 'My God'. The last tableau must be held for a few moments: the miners group round Joe, their hats in their hands, their rejoicing turned to silent mourning, as the tapping and singing of the rescuers get louder.

TALKING POINTS

On Staging and Acting

1. What directions would you give the actors in this play to help them to give the impression of being inside a confined space with low roof and irregular walls?
2. Consider how you would place the lamps and light the scene so as to suggest the inside of a mine.
3. How would you try to bring out the different sides of Dick's character in action – firstly, in his opening dialogue with Billie, secondly, in his argument with Peter, thirdly, in his remarks to Bob, and lastly, in his talk with Joe? Consider gestures, looks, and movements, as well as tone of voice.
4. In the second scene, Dick is described as being 'master of the situation'. Select passages which best show him in command and say how you think these should be spoken. Consider pace and tone as well as the emphasizing of words.
5. How would you direct the last scene to bring out the tragedy that takes place alongside or within the drama of the rescue?

On the Human Situation

1. Support a claim that this play should be considered as 'literature'.
2. What to them is important in the lives of these 'simple people'?
3. Dick's philosophy of life is the bedrock of the play.

What are the wrong attitudes that are shattered on this rock?

4. The conflicts come thick and fast. Contrast those in Scene One with those in Scene Two.

5. How are the characters changed by their experiences?

APPENDIX I

Producing a Play in School

Plays are written to be acted. The best way to get to know a play is to prepare it for a performance. In preparing it you will have a lot of hard work, you will have a lot of fun, and you will learn a lot about the theatre.

When you put on a play you aim at engaging the full attention of the audience. You must present it in the most finished and arresting form you can, within the limitations imposed on you by circumstances. And the problems to be solved in bringing a play to public performance are basically the same for a shoestring amateur or a well-financed professional company or for a group in a school. A worthwhile production takes shape only as a result of the co-ordinated efforts of many people, each one doing his particular job – and learning something about theatre craft as he does it.

Any producer of school plays will soon find that almost everyone has some kind of talent that can be used; a glance at the 'credits' on a programme gives an idea of some of the skills that have to be drawn on. To illustrate this we have arranged an outline of the duties associated with each person in a production team. In doing so we have had in mind a full-scale performance. We realize that in performances by school societies or by classes a much smaller team may be used, but we suggest that it is valuable for as many pupils as possible to be made to feel part of a production.

In outlining and commenting on the various duties we have in mind a producer and a team in school who are beginners in play production and performance. The hints aim at letting them see their jobs and preventing them from making the more obvious errors either during the preparation or on the occasion of a play's performance.

The Producer or Director
At the centre of any theatrical production is the *producer* or *director*. In school productions he has to assemble, direct and collaborate with a whole team of people, usually pupils and staff.

The Producer's Prompt Copy
The play chosen, the producer has to read the play until he knows it thoroughly and has decided how he can best bring out its special qualities on a stage. If it is a comedy, as *Rory Aforesaid*, he will look for ways of making an audience laugh, if a thriller, as *Thread o' Scarlet*, for ways of making them feel puzzlement, horror and suspense (see Production Notes for each play in this book). His next move is the preparation of a Producer's Prompt Copy; he can either paste each page of the text into a blank exercise book or interleave the playbook itself with blank sheets of the same size. Either way he will have space to jot down in words and diagrams the moves, grouping, entries and exits and stage business he wants to include. In Appendix II you will find as a model two pages for *Campbell of Kilmohr*. It is also a sound plan for a producer to encourage his players to jot down on *their* copies notes of moves and stage business.

Casting
We cannot always follow the instructions of the playwright as to height and colouring of his characters, but in general the producer will consider, when casting, the kind of looks, voice and build of his pupils and so get as near as possible to the

character conveyed by the author. Above all he should feel that any player is 'right' for the part. He should try, also, to provide for contrasts in physical appearance (in addition to the aid given by costume) so that characters are readily identifiable by the audience.

Rehearsals

The producer should have a rehearsal schedule that makes the minimum demands on pupils' time. No player should be asked to attend a rehearsal unless required – and rehearsed. The producer should first of all make his way systematically through the script, working out and explaining the shape of each sequence or episode until he has 'blocked in' the whole play, that is, shown all the important moves, entries and exits and groupings. In the subsequent rehearsals he should concentrate on ease of movement, fluent interpretation of speech, and varieties of pace. Every time he has taken players through one sequence or episode, he should give the cast the opportunity of playing it through without interruption. The dress rehearsal should be allowed to flow smoothly.

It is important that the producer impress on his cast that any schedule can only work well if the cast attending know their words and moves and are aware of the effect they are trying to put over. Only when the cast knows thoroughly what to do with their words can they do stage 'business' or move about the stage with freedom.

Costume

Hiring costumes is expensive, especially in period drama. In school, ingenuity is the keynote, and it is surprising what can be assembled through pupils and what a little skilful adaptation can do. The producer should try to provide costumes that suit the character *and* actor, to arrange different costumes for easy identification by the audience, and to give himself different colours for grouping. The state of the costumes, new or worn, splendid or decrepit, should answer the demands of the play.

Speech

The regional speech or 'accent' of pupils sometimes gives producers of school plays unnecessary worry. Of the five plays in this book, not one *requires* any special kind of accent for a local audience. The two golden rules for school productions are that the actors speak clearly and speak naturally.

For clarity, the producer has to get pupils accustomed to enunciating clearly and using a voice-volume that can be heard without strain by everyone in the auditorium. They must be trained to speak more deliberately than in everyday conversation, but with interesting and appropriate variations in tone, tempo, pitch and stress, so that they make meaningful patterns of sound. They must become sensitive to the value of pause, particularly the dramatic pause with its often quite lengthy silence. By slight pauses before and after a word or phrase, they can 'point' it. The producer can use the pause for building up tension, reducing it, suggesting a change of mood or a new situation. On the other hand young players must learn to pick cues up quickly to increase pace.

For 'naturalness' the producer should accept as his norm for English the kind of speech acceptable in the language exchange between pupil and teacher in the classroom; for Scots, the local Scots speech. If, of course, there are pupils who have the resources for other kinds of speech, these may be used for appropriate characters to provide welcome variety and contrast.

Noises Off

All noises off, except for the voices of persons in the play, should be pre-recorded on tape and when played in performance must be precisely timed for full effect.

The Stage

The producer must always keep in mind that his presentation is a form of communication. To give his audience an illusion of reality he has at his command a static inanimate scene inhabited by living players who move and speak.

(a) *The Set*. Depending on circumstances the producer may decide to use for his set curtains only, with a 'prop' or two to suggest the play's background. He may use a 'box' set and, if so, should remember that the 'props' indicated by the dramatist are usually of a functional kind. The details to fill out the picture have to be thought out and added. For example the details in *Campbell of Kilmohr* would suggest the grinding harshness of the living conditions. The producer may also use platforms to give different levels where appropriate to allow himself greater opportunities for significant positioning of his actors. But whatever arrangement of the set is decided on, adequate playing space must be left for the players to work in.

(b) *Lighting*. The set has to be lit. The producer is responsible for making out a lighting plot, that is the pattern of changes in brightness and colour. By skilful use of lighting he can reinforce at any point in the play the dramatic situation, the atmosphere or the importance of a particular character.

(c) *Positions on the Stage*. The school producer should familiarize his cast with the accepted terms used in stage directions – a shorthand method of indicating positions. They are shown in this diagram.

As a general rule the most commanding positions an actor can occupy lie in a line down the centre of the stage – Up C, C, Down C – the position becoming weaker as the actor is moved towards the wings. The producer thus has guide lines for arranging his characters

```
Up R      Up RC      Up C      Up LC      Up L


RC                    C                    LC


DC                  Down C                 DL
```

in a meaningful pattern during a scene or an episode; but for important long asides or soliloquies (rare in one-act plays) he may find other positions effective, for example the proscenium corner. He will soon learn how to effect a resounding entry, how to fade characters off from weaker positions, and where to tuck characters away from the audience's attention as, for example, he has to do with Morag Stewart for a time in *Campbell of Kilmohr*.

(d) *Grouping.* In any play the relative importance of characters changes as the sequence of episodes unfolds. Such alterations in dramatic status can be conveyed to the audience by new groupings of the actors. Of those on stage that character who is the focal point of interest in the episode should have the most commanding position on the stage. When the dramatic interest is shared between two characters they can be placed so as to give them equal or nearly equal status. In a school situation the producer should look out for three production points. First, he must avoid 'masking'; each character, when speaking, has to be seen by every member of the audience. Second, wherever a character is, and no matter to whom the character is speaking, he must be trained to remember that his main business is to speak to the audience. Third, the changing alliances in a play can be indicated by grouping and re-grouping; for example the isolation of a character with everyone against him, as in the ending of *Thread o' Scarlet*, or the triumph of *Rory Aforesaid*.

(e) *Actions*. One of the most difficult problems for pupil actors is what to do with their hands. Appropriate gesture is very effective dramatically, but the safest rule is that as little gesture should be done as possible, and that only if justified by the text. There is no substitute for practising in front of a mirror, and pupils should learn to time their actions, *usually* the gesture coming a fraction before the words that give rise to it. The one-act text normally indicates the 'business' to be done, but the producer, where he feels more is required, can always invent bits of his own. One last point: actors should be trained to begin acting a few moments before they actually appear on stage so that they are in character as soon as the audience catches sight of them. If they have to strut they must *appear* strutting, if shuffling they must *appear* shuffling.

(f) *Curtains*. No producer should leave curtain calls to chance. A performance is not over until the curtain comes down for the last time and the house lights are up. So the cast must be disciplined to hold their positions at the final curtain, not glancing at it while it closes. The speed of its closing will be determined by the producer and will vary according to the kind of play or the kind of ending of the play. All movements and groupings for curtain calls should be carefully rehearsed and at a performance should be adhered to rigidly.

The Stage Manager

The stage manager is in complete control of performances. He has to see to it that everything is in accordance with the producer's plan and he is there to help the actors to concentrate on their acting. He has to make sure that the lights and set are in order and that the actors are called, correctly dressed and with their 'props', ready for their entry. He has to arrange that all 'props' are assembled ready for use, that the prompter is in position, and the 'effects' team at their station.

A stage manager can be efficient only if he has a close knowledge of the text and of the producer's directions, grouping and so on. He should have been present at all 'company' rehearsals, taking notes of what, for his purposes, is needed so that he can form an overall picture of the staging needs of the play.

In school productions it is most important that he ensure that everybody engaged in the performance knows the difference between the stage area and the back-stage area. He should make certain that in the stage area there are only those assistants required for the smooth running of the play and that all of the people back-stage keep to their allotted quarters so that they can be summoned at a moment's notice. Above all, he should make sure the performance begins at the advertised time. To assist him carry out his duties he has a team. So that as many pupils as possible can get experience it is profitable to allocate separate teams or individuals to the various jobs; But if numbers are limited, two or more of these jobs may have to be undertaken by members of the team.

The Stage Crew

The size of this group varies according to the elaborateness of the set, the number of changes of scene and the length of interval time available. It should be as small as possible. A single performance of any of the one-act plays in this book presents few difficulties, since the set can be arranged at any time before the curtain rises. But if three one-act plays are presented as a single entertainment, the crew has to be more scrupulously organized and drilled.

The stage hands, in old clothes and 'sneakers', should have learned where the various pieces of the set are, who is to move which, the order in which they are to be moved, the entrances through which they are to be taken and the exact position (indicated by little chalk marks on the floor) they have to occupy. Similar arrangements should operate, but in reverse order of procedure, for striking the set. As the actors have definite positions to take up in the play and may have to perform rapid movements, the scene must be set accurately. And, as sounds travel through a curtain, even a heavy one, the stage crew must accustom themselves to working quietly as well as quickly. They should not leave the stage until the stage manager, whose duty it is to oversee their work, has made his final check and releases them until their next call. The stage manager must pay special attention to hidden 'props' that have to be taken from the inside of cupboards; or for example the box in *The Pardoner's Tale*.

The Cast

The stage manager has to check in good time that all actors have arrived and are fit to perform. He will have fixed the times at which the players and their understudies have to arrive. The cast must be meticulous time-keepers, even if some of them are not required on stage till later in a full-length play. Understudies should not be freed until their principals have reported.

All members of the cast are responsible for their own costumes and for any 'personal props', that is, for whatever they may have to wear or to carry each time they are on stage. They should ensure that they are complete in costume and make-up ten to fifteen minutes before they are due to make their first entrance. Where such effects as wetness or snow have to appear on costumes, as for example in *Campbell of*

Kilmohr, Thread o' Scarlet and *The Pardoner's Tale*, the stage manager must make the necessary arrangements and see that they have been carried out.

The Make-Up Team

Except in large-scale ventures such as an opera or a full-length play with numerous walk-on parts, and certainly in all one-act plays in this book, no elaborate make-up team is needed. It is always an advantage, and especially if expertise is required, to have someone give a general talk on the art of stage make-up. Such a talk can help to avoid at least some of the worst mistakes that can interfere with the audience's illusion. Talks on make-up should not be difficult to arrange for schools in Scotland. There are knowledgeable amateurs in S.C.D.A. groups all over the country, and some favourably placed schools can ask assistance from the nearest repertory companies, who are usually well disposed towards helping shcools with professional expertise. Thus all players can learn how to put on the basic stage make-up, leaving the finer points to the make-up team.

'Props' Master

In most plays in addition to the 'personal props' for which the actors are individually responsible, there are 'props' which have to be taken on by the actors for part of a scene only or part of a play only; for example MacCallum's papers in *Rory Aforesaid* or the loaded tray for the Traveller in *Thread o' Scarlet*. Generally these are kept on a suitably sized, suitably placed table in the wings or, if space permits, near the entrance to the stage area. Before and after the performance the 'props' man must check that the 'props' are complete and that they are neatly arranged, preferably in the order of time in which they are needed in the play. The actors come to collect such 'props' before going on stage and hand them back immediately they come off. The stage manager must see to it that the 'props' are in order and ready.

Call Boy

In a one-act play only one call boy is necessary. Except when notifying the actors he keeps close to the stage manager, who will tell him whom to call and when. At such times he goes to the dressing-room and tells the actor *by the name he or she has in the play* the time they have before appearing: for example, 'Dugald Stewart, two minutes.' In school productions it is best for the call boy to accompany the actor to the entrance point before reporting to the stage manager who can then check on the actor. But whether a call-system is in operation or not it is the duty of each player to be on the *qui vive* for all his entries.

Lighting Crew

The lighting group, with someone in charge to give directions, will have made up their own lighting schedule in accordance with the producer's plan. Whatever the variations in lighting that are called for, it is the crew's business, having rehearsed them previously, to effect all changes as unobtrusively as possible, so that the audience do not become aware, at any moment of time, that a change is in process of taking place.

The lighting crew may also be in charge of 'House' lights, if these are controllable from the stage switchboard. So with lights set for the opening scene they await the stage manager's 'House lights down'. Thereafter they make all changes on their own until the order 'House lights up'. Before leaving the switchboard they have to arrange the lighting for the opening of the next performance, if there is one.

Curtain Hand

Many school and amateur performances have opened or

closed badly because of faulty curtain operations. The curtain operator, who takes his orders directly from the stage manager, must make sure beforehand that the mechanism works properly. He must know and be able to put into effect the exact curtain speeds demanded by the producer. He must be ready, if a fixed schedule has not been made for curtain calls, to provide at once on instruction from the stage manager, the curtain speeds called for.

Prompter

The prompter sits in the prompt corner, traditionally on the actors' left as they face the audience. The prompter must always be in such a position that the actors on stage can see him and he can see them. He should have attended enough rehearsals for him to know not only the text but the action on stage and all the dramatic pauses. Thus if an actor departs from the routine of the play the prompter should have no hesitation in supplying a cue *in a voice which the actors can hear clearly and at once*.

APPENDIX II

Producer's Prompt Copy
Extract from Campbell of Kilmohr

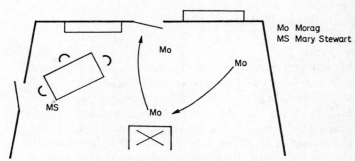

Mo Morag
MS Mary Stewart

1. Morag lights candle and places it at window back L.
2. Morag puts out candle and places plaid in front of fire. She quickly glides to door C back and opens it. Enter Dugald Stewart C back. He comes forward.
3. Morag, on Dugald's right, places her hand on his arm or shoulder. Mary Stewart uncovers fire, moves L, and re-lights candle. She comes to Dugald's left.
4. Mary Stewart comes close to Dugald, leads him to the fire door C. He sits on stool. Morag moves down R a little.
5. Mary places hand on Dugald's arm and turns head in Morag's direction.
6. Morag goes out at door R to barn.

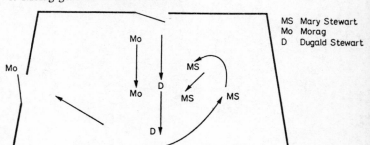

MS Mary Stewart
Mo Morag
D   Dugald Stewart

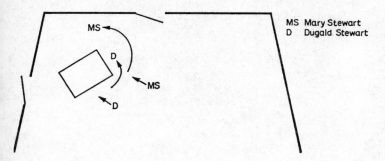

1. Dugald rises and moves a little up R. Mary Stewart follows.
2. Dugald close to Mary again. Both are standing.
3. Dugald goes to chair left of table and sits. Mary goes to cupboard back R and places food on table.
4. Morag re-enters from door R. She sits on chair right of table. Mary Stewart sits on chair behind table.

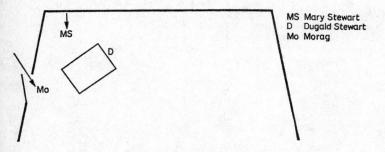